The Future of Organized Labor in American Politics

Peter L. Francia

The Future of Organized Labor in American Politics

COLUMBIA UNIVERSITY PRESS NEW YORK

Columbia University Press
Publishers Since 1893
New York   Chichester, West Sussex

Library of Congress Cataloging-in-Publication Data

Francia, Peter L.
The future of organized labor in American politics / Peter L. Francia.
p. cm.
Includes bibliographical references and index.
ISBN 0–231–13070–8 (cloth : alk. paper)—0–231–50393–8 (e-book)
1. Labor unions—United States—Political activity.
2. Politics, Practical—United States. 3. Elections—United States. I title.

HD6510.F73 2006
324.7'088'33188—dc22   2005049746

Columbia University Press books are printed
on permanent and durable acid-free paper.

Printed in the United States of America

c 10 9 8 7 6 5 4 3 2 1

Contents

Preface

THE ROOTS OF this study trace back to the summer of 1993, when District Council 37 in New York City gave me my first political job as an intern, assisting with political activities for the upcoming mayoral and city council races of that year. The experience served as a catalyst in developing my interest in unions and their effect on American elections and politics. Shortly after that summer, I intently followed organized labor's unsuccessful campaign to stop the passage of the North American Free Trade Agreement (NAFTA) in 1993, and its inability in preventing the Republicans' landslide congressional victories in 1994.

Like many political observers, I began to wonder if unions still mattered in American politics. Were unions still capable of regrouping, adapting, and reversing the tide against them? I watched with great interest in 1995 when the AFL-CIO elected John Sweeney its new president. I was initially skeptical that Sweeney and his slate of "New Voice" leaders truly represented a new direction for the American labor movement. I was even more skeptical that they would be capable of reversing labor's declining political fortunes, particularly given the Republicans' takeover of Congress.

Following Sweeney's election, organized labor appeared to be on the rebound in American politics. The Sweeney administration implemented a number of changes in labor's political strategies and tactics, including a renewed emphasis on grassroots activism. These changes contributed to a large union household turnout in the 1996 and 1998 elections. While Democrats failed to win back majorities in Congress in 1996 and 1998, organized labor's reinvigorated political operations played a critical role in a number of competitive congressional races, and ultimately helped Democrats gain seats in the House of Representatives and the U.S. Senate.

In the aftermath of the 1996 and 1998 elections, I became convinced that the predictions of labor's demise, which followed the Democrats' crushing defeat in the 1994 election, were not only premature, but wrong. With its energized ground war, labor had effectively countered the efforts of their political opponents. As I began to write about the "renaissance" of organized labor in American politics, labor's opponents regrouped. The Democrats in the House of Representatives gained seats in 2000, but the White House went to Republican George W. Bush—albeit in controversial fashion. Republicans in the House of Representatives and the U.S. Senate, however, added to their slim majorities in 2002, despite the historical trend that the party of the incumbent president loses seats in midterm congressional elections. The 2004 election brought the most devastating results for organized labor in a decade, with President George W. Bush winning reelection and Republicans securing their majorities in both chambers of Congress.

Following the Republicans' successes in the 2000, 2002, and 2004 elections, the labor movement is at a critical stage in its history—a stage similar to where it was following the 1994 elections. As it did after that election, the labor movement will again need to regroup if it is to remain a viable political force in the United States. In particular, organized labor must reverse the continued declines in union membership as a percentage of the American workforce. While organizing workers into unions is often thought of in terms of its effect on workers' rights, wages, benefits, and empowerment at the workplace, organizing efforts have significant political implications as well. As the results in this book will demonstrate, unions can effectively counter the financial power of business with manpower. The Sweeney administration deserves an enormous amount of credit for recognizing the importance of grassroots campaigning and for its ability to increase voter turnout in union households. As the evidence in this book will make clear, several union-endorsed candidates won election to the U.S. House and U.S. Senate, which may not have been possible absent the grassroots efforts of organized labor.

While labor's invigorated grassroots campaign efforts under John Sweeney have been a promising development, the labor movement has failed to achieve its overriding goal of helping the Democratic Party regain a majority in the U.S. House and the U.S. Senate. Unions are certainly not to blame for the failures of the Democratic Party. However, the results of the 2000, 2002, and 2004 elections make clear that mobilizing members at present levels of union density is simply not enough. Labor must expand its ranks if it is to remain a viable political force.

While the inspiration for the subject of this book came from my own early experience in the labor movement, this work would not have been possible without the assistance of many important people and institutions. To begin with, I owe a special debt of gratitude to Professor Paul S. Herrnson, the Director of the Center for American Politics and Citizenship at the University of Maryland, College Park. No single person has been more helpful to my professional career than Paul. He advised and guided me through numerous research projects while I was a student at the University of Maryland and a research fellow at the Center for American Politics and Citizenship. His advice on this project was particularly helpful. I will always be most thankful to Paul for providing me with almost instant feedback and suggestions on various portions of this book. Paul often put my work ahead of his own, and for that I will always be grateful.

I wish to thank the Department of Political Science at East Carolina University. All of my ECU colleagues have been supportive of my work and have offered helpful advice on this book when I needed it. Several of my colleagues have noted the irony of my interest in unions and the fact that I now work and live in North Carolina—the least unionized state in the nation. While there is no denying the weakness of organized labor in North Carolina, there is also no denying that I have had the good fortune of working with knowledgeable labor colleagues. The Department of Political Science at East Carolina University has truly been a congenial and stimulating place to conduct my research and work.

I also wish to thank Professors James Gimpel, Alan Neustadtl, and Eric Uslaner of the University of Maryland, Professor Clyde Wilcox of Georgetown University, and Professor Kelly Patterson of Brigham Young University, each of whom offered useful suggestions during the early stages of this study's research. Professor Kenneth Goldstein at the University of Wisconsin deserves acknowledgment for providing me with data from the Campaign Media Analysis Group on the AFL-CIO's advertising campaign during the 2000 and 2002 elections. Likewise, the staff at Peter D. Hart Research Associates was extremely cooperative, providing me with exit poll data of union members for this project.

Professor Eric S. Heberlig of the University of North Carolina, Charlotte, deserves special mention for reading and commenting on the initial draft of this book. His thoughtful suggestions greatly improved the quality of the final manuscript. Nathan Bigelow and Timothy Daly of the University of Maryland also read the initial draft of the book manuscript. Their attention to detail proved to be extremely helpful. I am further indebted to the Pew Charitable Trusts, which helped fund some of the initial research in this study through its support of the Campaign Assessment and Candidate Outreach Project. Two students at the University of Maryland, Julia Clements and Kelly Kolson, collected some of the candidate data for this project and deserve acknowledgment for their hard work and assistance.

I am especially grateful to members of the labor community who helped me with this project. Neal Kwatra, who is a close friend of mine and serves as a research analyst for UNITE HERE, deserves special mention for encouraging me to pursue this topic and for offering firsthand knowledge of labor's campaign activities in the 1996 through 2004 elections. Susan Dundon of the AFL-CIO and the staff at the George Meany Center for Labor Studies in Silver Spring, Maryland, were helpful in assisting me track down various pieces of important information. Susan Phillips of the United Food and Commercial International Union was particularly generous. She helped arrange my interview with John Pérez of the California Labor Federation and sent me useful materials on the Proposition 226 campaign in California to aid my research.

Everyone at Columbia University Press has been a pleasure to work with in preparing this book. I wish to thank Professor Robert Shapiro of Columbia University for making this book a part of his series, "Power, Conflict, and Democracy: American Politics into the Twenty-first Century." I also wish to acknowledge Peter Dimock, senior executive editor at Columbia University Press, whose assistance was vital to this book's completion. On a very sad note, John Michel, who served as the original editor of this manuscript, passed away before this book's completion. John's advice and suggestions were instrumental in the early stages of the book's progress. I will miss him.

I leave my last thanks to my family. My mother, father, and brother have always provided me with support when I most needed it. Indeed, they are more than family to me—they are my best friends. I leave my warmest and deepest appreciation to my wife, Kali, who helped edit this manuscript and even helped me look up several facts and figures for this book. Her research assistance was as helpful to me as her emotional support. Kali tolerated numerous inconveniences to accommodate my efforts to complete this book. Her patience and encouragement were invaluable to me during this project.

Finally, I dedicate this book to my four grandparents. My mother's parents, Joe and Lucy, passed away when I was very young. While I did not get to know them, their lives exemplified the hard work and sacrifice that so many American workers face today. My grandfather, an Italian immigrant and union member, worked two jobs as a boilermaker and carpenter to support his six children. His spirit lives in this book. My father's parents, Frank and Rose Francia, were two of the most important influences in my life. My grandfather had a deep respect for education, and always

The Future of Organized Labor in American Politics

Let the workers organize. Let the toilers assemble. Let their crystallized voice proclaim their injustices and demand their privileges. Let all thoughtful citizens sustain them, for the future of labor is the future of America.[1]

—JOHN LEWIS, PRESIDENT OF THE CIO (1935–1940)

1

Introduction

JOHN LEWIS, THE president of the Congress of Industrial Organizations (CIO) from 1935 to 1940, once proclaimed that the "future of Labor is the future of America" (Selvin 1969).[2] In the 1950s, President Dwight D. Eisenhower observed that "unions have a secure place in our industrial life. Only a handful of reactionaries harbor the ugly thought of breaking unions and depriving working men and women of the right to join the union of their choice" (American Labor Studies Center 2004).

By the end of the century, however, the perceptions of organized labor had dramatically changed. Unions no longer represented the future of America, nor did they have a secure place in industrial life (Piven and Cloward 1982; Goldfield 1987; Moody 1988; Sexton 1991). The decades of the 1980s and 1990s were particularly difficult for organized labor. One scholar described those years as "among the worst in this century for unions and workers" (Mantsios 1998, xv). During the mid-1990s, one columnist wrote that the American labor movement had "never been weaker in its 113-year-old history" (Beichman 1994). Those within labor's ranks even offered harsh criticisms. In 1995, the president of the National Writers Union wrote: "For too many years, the labor movement has been called a dinosaur. This is unfair and almost slanderous—not for labor, but for the poor, maligned dinosaur" (Tasini 1995).

These disparaging descriptions of the American labor movement were the result of nearly a half-century of scandals, setbacks, and defeats for unions. By the mid-1990s, unions had experienced a steady and precipitous four-decade drop in unionization rates. Union density, which reached a height of one of every three workers in the nonagricultural workforce in 1955, fell to less than one of every seven workers four decades later (Bureau of Labor Statistics 2005). By comparison, other Western industrial democracies, such as Canada, Great Britain, and Germany, all had rates of unionization roughly twice as high as the United States (ILR 2003).

Union workers also experienced a decline in their living standards during the 1970s and beyond. Businesses that once offered secure jobs to low-skilled workers closed their factories in the United States, taking advantage of cheaper labor costs in other nations (Lichtenstein 2002). Strikes, once a common and important weapon in labor's arsenal to win better wages and benefits for workers, decreased in number dramatically in the 1990s and the early twenty-first century. Work stoppages involving 1,000 or more workers topped the 400 mark several times from the 1950s through the 1970s. By comparison, the number of strikes involving 1,000 or more workers in the 1990s was below fifty for the entire decade (see figure 1.1).

Real wages declined for the working class through much of the 1970s, 1980s, and first half of the 1990s, falling 15 percent from 1973 to 1995 (Brecher and Costello 1998, 25). During the same period, CEO salaries reached new heights. In 1975, the CEO of General Electric earned a salary roughly equivalent to that of thirty-six working families. By 1995, that number increased to 133 families (Barlett and Steele 1996, 19). A single CEO in the 1990s earned more in a single year than the combined average income of sixty-five workers over the course of their lifetimes (Mantsios 1998, xvi).

Along with the worsening of workers' economic situations, labor's political influence suffered a major blow in 1994, when the

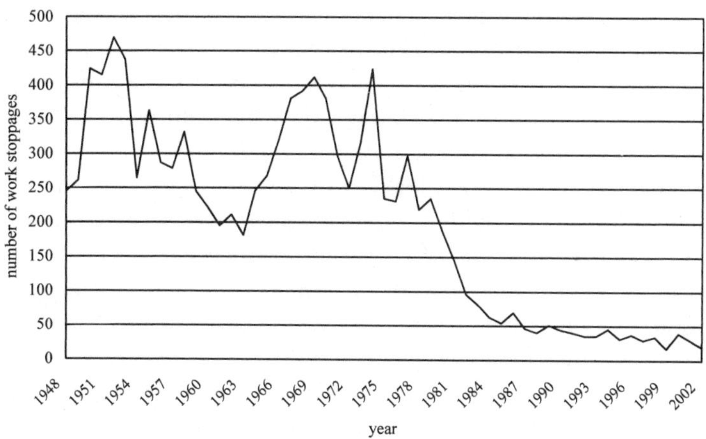

FIGURE 1.1 Work Stoppages Involving 1,000 Workers or More, 1948–2002
Source: Bureau of Labor Statistics.

Republican Party won majorities in both chambers of Congress for the first time in four decades. The incoming Speaker of the House, Newt Gingrich, chided union leaders as "big labor bosses" (Roman 1997). Dick Armey, the new majority leader, opposed basic labor law protections such as the minimum wage. He once stated: "This [minimum wage] is bad public policy. . . . The fact is, raising the minimum wage is going to destroy job opportunities. . . . It is a cruel hoax on the least advantaged workers in the system. . . . I taught economics in colleges for a lot of years; any freshmen who didn't get it, didn't pass" (Yang and Chandler 1996).

Before the Republicans' victory, labor had enjoyed relatively easy access to the Democratic leadership and had built close relationships with the chairmen of important committees. A simple but symbolic illustration of labor's access was the allowing of union lobbyists to make telephone calls in a suite of offices in the Capitol occupied by the doorkeeper, Jim Malloy (Gerber 1999, 79). While unions often failed to win major reforms in labor law, even under Democratic control of Congress, they could generally depend on Democrats as the last line of defense in stopping assaults on workers' rights. Harold Meyerson (1998, 4) explains: "So long as the Democrats held the House, pro-union committee chairmen would bottle up whatever union-busting brainstorms and bludgeoning of the welfare state bubbled forth from Newt Gingrich and other Hill Republicans."

However, the Republicans' victory put organized labor on the defensive. Unions could no longer push for labor law reform. Instead, they now faced an emboldened business community that pledged to push for an overhaul of numerous labor regulations, notably the Fair Labor Standards Act, which sets the minimum wage and other salary-related issues (Mills and Swoboda 1994). As Taylor Dark (1999, 179) describes, "with the loss of the House in 1994, labor was suddenly thrust into its most perilous political situation since the passage of the Taft-Hartley Act in 1947."

The task to rebuild the shattered labor movement fell largely on the shoulders of the American Federation of Labor–Congress of Industrial Organizations, the largest labor organization in the United States, with a membership of more than thirteen million workers. Given the crisis that the labor movement confronted, the conditions were ripe for organizational change. In February 1995, leaders of the AFL-CIO held a closed-door, executive council meeting in Bal Harbour, Florida, to debate whether to replace their president, Lane Kirkland, who had held the office since 1979.

The opposition to Kirkland included three major groups: the manufacturing unions (e.g., the United Auto Workers, the Steelworkers, and the Mineworkers), the public sector unions (e.g., the American Federation of State, County, and Municipal Employees and the Service Employees International Union), and the Teamsters. These unions represented a sizable faction, combining to represent more than 40 percent of the AFL-CIO's membership. Initially, this opposition bloc encouraged Thomas Donahue, the secretary-treasurer of the AFL-CIO, to challenge Kirkland for the presidency. Donahue resisted the overtures, deciding instead to remain loyal to Kirkland, who had elevated him to his secretary-treasurer position. The opposition ultimately turned to John J. Sweeney, the president of the Service Employees International Union, who agreed to oppose Kirkland.

During Sweeney's tenure as president of the SEIU, membership doubled to more than 1.1 million workers (although most of the increase came from mergers of existing local unions; see Buhle 1999, 45). Sweeney, however, was willing to resort to acts of civil disobedience to bring attention to the cause of his members. In September 1995, Sweeney led a blockade of the Roosevelt Bridge in Washington, D.C., on behalf of organizing efforts for janitors (Swoboda 1995a). Sweeney campaigned for the presidency of the AFL-CIO on a platform dubbed the "New Voice for American Workers," which promised a more confrontational labor movement. He criticized the existing leadership's ineffectiveness and "deafening silence" on important union issues (Brecher 1997, 346).

Through May 1995, Kirkland still commanded the support of twenty-one union leaders, who collectively represented more than four million convention votes. However, his opposition was growing. Some of the major building trade unions, including the Carpenters, Operating Engineers, Painters, and Sheet Metal Workers and the powerful United Food and Commercial Workers, joined the resistance to Kirkland. Gerald McEntee, president of the American Federation of State, County, and Municipal Employees, noted that the opposition had built a majority. As he bluntly remarked, "It doesn't take a rocket scientist to figure out we've got 53 percent of the votes" (Swoboda 1995b).

Recognizing that defeat was imminent, Kirkland announced that he would step down as president on June 12, 1995. Ironically, the opposition's first choice to oppose Kirkland, Thomas Donahue, declared his candidacy for the AFL-CIO presidency shortly after Kirkland's announcement. Kirkland named Donahue the interim president of the AFL-CIO following his retirement. Donahue campaigned on a moderate platform and was sharply critical of Sweeney's aggressive methods, stating that unions "must worry less about blocking bridges and worry more about building bridges for the rest of society" (Swoboda 1995a).

After a contentious campaign, Sweeney won the support of unions representing 7.3 million workers to Donahue's support from unions representing 5.6 million workers. By some accounts, Sweeney's victory symbolized a changing of the guard from labor's conservative forces to its progressive factions. Indeed, Sweeney's "New Voice" coalition included a generation of progressive, "New Left" leaders, many of whom had been involved in the antiwar and civil rights protests of the 1960s and 1970s. As Taylor Dark (1999, 183) explains: "Paradoxically, given the more conservative tenor of American politics in general, the victory of the Sweeney coalition also registered the triumph of the more liberal—even social democratic—wing of the labor movement for the first time in the history of the federation."

In a news conference following his victory, Sweeney vowed to reverse labor's decline by creating a "new" AFL-CIO that would refocus its resources on organizing, political education, and lobbying activities. His political action plan included expanded get-out-the-vote activities and a high-profile issue advertising campaign. Sweeney and his team of leaders at the AFL-CIO also adopted a more aggressive political tone, threatening to punish members of Congress who voted against their interests. "We are doing things differently [than in the past], so that [politicians] don't forget, and those that do forget ultimately pay a price," remarked Richard Trumka, the secretary-treasurer of the AFL-CIO (Victor and Carney 1999, 2482).

Despite the strong rhetoric, some labor scholars have been skeptical that Sweeney has brought about the changes necessary to rebuild the labor movement. Paul Buhle (1999, 1) writes that at the time of Sweeney's election, "labor conservatives gnashed their teeth, and radicals of all generations responded with enthusiasm and hope. The first years after these developments have not, however, been kind to utopian dreamers." In a similar vein, Jane Slaughter (1999, 50) notes that the "politics of the union hierarchy have not changed. The New Voice team remains committed to the same stance towards employers and to the same methods of functioning that helped organized labor to its current puny proportion of the workforce."

Others argue that the political policies of unions have remained fundamentally and principally unchanged. They cite labor's continued support of "less than progressive" Democrats and the little influence labor had on President Bill Clinton's second-term agenda, despite its active support during his reelection campaign (Brecher and Costello 1999, 15; Buhle 1999, 2). Others note that labor's political strategies remain "cemented" in pragmatism and tied to the Democratic Party, as evidenced by the AFL-CIO's reluctance to publicize its opposition to welfare reform in 1996 (Aronowitz 1998, 189–190).

In contrast, some researchers have offered praise for Sweeney. One author writes, "The new AFL-CIO is giving working people a fighting chance, putting to the test—every single day—practical ways to curb corporate power and to strengthen the hand of the working people" (Mort 1998, x). Another assessment noted that the Sweeney administration offered "new hope," with "revitalization now at the top of the agenda for a once demoralized labor movement" (Turner, Katz, and Hurd 2001, 2).

These conflicting assessments illustrate the disagreement that remains over labor's direction since Sweeney's victory. The purpose of this book is to contribute to this debate, focusing primarily on congressional politics. Political action in congressional elections has been a major component of the AFL-CIO's revitalization strategy, and an assessment of its successes in the political arena is an important element in determining whether unions have begun to reverse, or at least stem, their decline. Indeed, a systematic analysis of organized labor's recent election activities is in order. As Margaret Levi (2003, 59) writes, "social scientists . . . have paid relatively little attention to the actual leverage of the recent labor vote and how well [labor's] current electoral strategy will work. These questions deserve serious scholarly investigation." This book is an attempt to fill that gap in the social science literature.

In evaluating the AFL-CIO's political program, I contend it is necessary to consider the Sweeney administration's success from a relative perspective. Would organized labor hold more, less, or about the same influence in congressional politics had the previous leadership remained in power? Against that standard, I argue that the Sweeney administration has improved labor's political influence in congressional politics. Indeed, the labor movement has not withered away as many in the mid-1990s expected it would. On the contrary, the Sweeney leadership has reorganized labor's political program since taking over the AFL-CIO. In particular, the Sweeney administration has countered the financial power of business by directing labor's resources into grassroots efforts to mobilize union members. These efforts were critical in the victories of several Democratic House and Senate candidates during Sweeney's tenure.

This is not to suggest that the Sweeney administration has had a perfect record or to diminish the challenges that continue to face organized labor. The consecutive victories of Republican George W. Bush to the White House in 2000 and 2004 and the Republicans' expanded majorities in the House and Senate following the 2002 and 2004 elections all suggest that labor must do more. Republican victories occurred despite significant efforts by organized labor to mobilize its existing membership. Thus, while unions have made progress under Sweeney, serious challenges remain. Chief among these challenges is the continuing decline of union workers as a percentage of the workforce. The mobilization of union members at present levels of union density is simply not enough. Labor must invest even more heavily in organizing efforts to increase its membership and ultimately its influence in American politics.

The Importance of Leadership for Political Organizations and Interest Groups

The Sweeney leadership's successes and failures not only have obvious implications for the labor movement, but also provide some broader lessons about the importance of leadership for political organizations and interest groups. While rank-and-file members are important given that political struggles cannot succeed without them, leaders are the ones who provide direction, control the organization's resources, and direct activities that move the group toward its goals. As Salisbury (1969) argues in his "exchange theory," groups decline when leaders fail to provide their members with material, solidary, or purposive benefits. Likewise, Mancur Olson (1971) points to the importance of leaders providing "selective benefits" (benefits that go only to group members and cannot be shared by nonmembers). Selective incentives, according to Olson, are the foundation upon which groups attract members and build their strength.

Even those skeptical of leaders' motives, such as Robert Michels—who argued in his theory on the "iron law of oligarchy" that leaders are primarily motivated not for the general will of the members they serve but for their own preservation of power—acknowledged the importance of leadership: "The incompetence of the masses is almost universal throughout the domains of political life, and this constitutes the most solid foundation of the power of the leaders. . . . Since the rank and file are incapable of looking after their own interests, it is necessary that they should have experts to attend to their affairs" (Michels [1910] 1962, 111–112).

Thus, the theoretical underpinning of this book is that leadership is critical to the strength of political organizations, and that a change in leadership can infuse new thinking and ideas necessary for a group to remain viable in a changing environment. New leadership can revitalize a stagnant organization by reexamining the needs of its members, exploring new tactics, and reaffirming the principles fundamental to the mission of the group. While the earlier theories outlined by Salisbury and Olsen focus on how leaders or "entrepreneurs" attract individuals to join their organizations, my focus is on how leaders are important in mobilizing their membership to build stronger political organizations in the electoral and legislative arenas. Indeed, the change in leadership at the AFL-CIO provides an instructive example of how leaders who are innovative and who adapt their group's strategies can have an important effect on the strength and influence of the organizations that they lead. It is therefore my hope that this book will have value not only to those who study organized labor, but also to those interested in leadership change and its effect on interest group influence in American politics.

Moreover, this book has a place in the emerging literature on campaign effects. Several studies from the 1990s reported that campaigns have a significant effect in elections at both the individual and aggregate levels (see, e.g., Ansolabehere and Iyengar 1995; Holbrook 1996; Shaw 1999; Herrnson 2004). These studies and other related works found that campaign efforts can affect voter turnout and have a marginal effect on how well candidates perform in elections.

Labor unions have long played an active role in congressional campaigns, providing candidates with contributions and other services. Unions have a well-known history of providing volunteers to campaigns and assisting campaigns with voter registration and get-out-the-vote drives. These campaign efforts are often significant in congressional elections. As I will demonstrate in this book, union campaign efforts, particularly during John Sweeney's tenure, have had an important effect in generating higher turnout and political participation among union members. These efforts have also had a significant effect on the outcomes of several House and Senate elections and in shaping congressional policies on labor legislation.

The Structure and Organization of Labor Unions

Labor unions are associations that promote and protect the welfare of workers. The term "organized labor" refers to the employees represented by unions. For the purpose of this book, "labor unions" and "organized labor" are terms that I use interchangeably.

The term "labor movement" has connotations with the idea of social movements. Social movements are broad, society-wide phenomena that challenge the traditional social order, typically working outside of existing institutional channels (Gamson 1975; Tarrow 1998; Form 2000). While unions often engage in social-disorder tactics, unions largely function to affect change within existing institutional channels, and have developed a bureaucratic set of organizations with very specific political alliances. Unions are thus largely classified as interest groups. As Asher and his colleagues (2001, 3–4) explain, "American labor unions have, over time, evolved from social movement status through social movement organizations into interest groups." The term "labor movement" therefore has meanings beyond the context of a social movement, and, in this book, is another term that is used interchangeably with "organized labor" and "unions."

Unions collectively represent more than sixteen million workers in the United States and negotiate on behalf of these workers for improved workplace safety, job security, pay, and benefits. Whether unions are necessary to provide those benefits to workers has been long debated. Critics of unions contend that they are corrupt, undemocratic, and function as monopolies in the labor market, which has a negative effect on the economy (Simons 1948; Machlup 1952; Friedman and Friedman 1980). Many corporate leaders denounce unions as "irrelevant" in the modern, high-tech, postindustrial economy (Lichtenstein 1999, 64), and as Goldfield (1987, 57) summarizes:

> For them [critics], trade unions are merely corrupt organizations led by dictatorial, high-salaried leaders, sheltering overpaid, lazy, featherbedding workers whose low productivity and defense of outdated work-rules hold back innovative technology, raising prices of both manufactured goods (e.g., cars, tires, steel, and appliances) and construction (homes, highways, and governmental buildings).

Defenders of organized labor often note that unions improve wages and build workers' morale by giving them a voice at the workplace (Slichter, Healy, and Livernash 1960; Bok and Dunlop 1970). In the political arena, unions function to provide a voice for workers in government. Most unions endorse candidates for various political offices and provide political assistance and resources to targeted campaigns. Unions lobby all levels of government to pass legislation that not only affects the economic self-interest of their members, but also has far-reaching social objectives, such as civil rights and the expansion of the welfare state (Marks 1989; Cornfield 1991).

The political activities of the AFL-CIO are particularly important. The AFL-CIO is the head of the labor movement and comprises a voluntary federation of sixty affiliated but autonomous unions. It charters 580 central labor councils and fifty-one state chapters (including Puerto Rico). The Central Labor Councils

(CLCs) comprise local AFL-CIO affiliates that are typically organized at the county level. Delegates from the locals hold CLC meetings to collect and disseminate information to union members, debate and vote on issues affecting unions, coordinate community activities, and recommend candidate endorsements to the state federation (Wilcox 1994, 22; Asher et al. 2001, 69). The CLCs and the state chapters of the AFL-CIO typically cooperate with their parent organization, the International, but also maintain their independence (Wright 1985; Ezra 1999, 95).

Although rare, the federated structure of organized labor can sometimes lead to splits within organized labor. In the 1998 New York Senate election, Republican Alfonse D'Amato received the backing of the Building and Construction Trades Council, while his opponent, Democrat Charles Schumer, won the endorsement of the Communications Workers of America and the SEIU. These internal divisions sometimes prevent organized labor from forging a united front in elections (Greenhouse 1998).

Other affiliated unions have a history of independence from the rest of the labor movement. The Teamsters spent roughly three decades outside of the AFL-CIO, and during that time they earned a reputation as a more politically conservative union. The Teamsters endorsed Republican presidential candidates Richard Nixon in 1972, Ronald Reagan in 1980 and 1984, and George H. W. Bush in 1988, in direct opposition to the national AFL-CIO leadership. During the 1984 election, Teamsters president Jackie Presser stated that the AFL-CIO's support of the Mondale-Ferraro presidential ticket created "an embarrassing situation for all of labor" (New York Times 1984).

Despite the independence of the local unions, the top leadership of the AFL-CIO still wields considerable influence over the entire labor movement. The AFL-CIO's Executive Council consists of the president, secretary-treasurer, executive vice-president, and fifty-one vice presidents. The president of the AFL-CIO is also the chief executive officer of the federation. According to the constitution of the AFL-CIO (Article X, Section 9), the president has the authority to provide direction, staff, and resources for organizational activities. These responsibilities provide the president with the power to shape the policies of the AFL-CIO and influence the direction of the labor movement.

Aside from these important formal responsibilities, the AFL-CIO president is also the national spokesman for the unions whose very image, actions, and personality can come to define organized labor. As Nelson Lichtenstein (2002, 247) explains:

> The top leadership of the AFL-CIO does more than simply preside over a confederation of autonomous unions. An AFL-CIO president speaks for organized labor to Congress, the White House, and the public. His institutional authority is considerable when it comes to labor's "foreign policy" and almost as weighty when domestic politics and economic policy are under debate. Moreover, a certain charisma attaches to the leader of an institution that claims to speak for 50 million family members whose livelihood is dependent on a unionized breadwinner.

Further evidence of the national leadership's importance is the lead role that the AFL-CIO's Committee on Political Education (COPE) has in the political arena. A COPE endorsement often signals other union political action committees to contribute to a candidate, which can translate into significant funds. In some congressional races, a COPE endorsement can trigger as much as $250,000 in early money to candidates (Wilcox 1994, 25).

Indeed, COPE is a highly active PAC in congressional elections. Although it is not the largest contributor among labor PACs, COPE is typically one of the twenty largest PAC contributors to Democratic congressional candidates, and it regularly outspends other Democratic-leaning organizations. In 2002, COPE spent $1.8 million in congressional elections, mainly to support Democrats. By comparison, the Sierra Club's PAC gave roughly $828,000, and the National Organization for Women's PAC gave slightly less than $305,000 (Center for Responsive Politics 2003).

Congressional candidates also can expect other benefits from COPE, notably communications assistance through telephone banks, direct mail, flyers, and direct contact by union members. COPE influences other labor PACs to contribute money to its endorsed candidates (Wilcox 1994, 19). Given the lead role that COPE plays in labor politics, the change in leadership at the AFL-CIO has obvious and important implications for the future of organized labor in congressional politics.

The Relevance of Unions in an Era of Decline

Perhaps the strongest indicator of union decline is the half-century drop in union density. Labor scholar Kim Moody (1988, 4) concludes that the decline in unionization "has had an inevitable correlate in a loss of union power in industry and society as a whole." Some note a connection between the declines in unionization and labor's political strength. As one team of scholars writes: "Lower levels of unionization have led to a loss in political power. . . . Today, with union density at its lowest point in sixty years, even the protective laws are under attack as never before" (Bronfenbrenner et al. 1998, 7).

Others contend that unions have become powerless in the face of an increasingly conservative or "rightward" political shift in the United States. Some cite the antiunion policies of Ronald Reagan in the 1980s and his ability to break the air traffic controllers' strike in 1981 as signs of organized labor's weakness (Rehmus 1984; Wilcox 1994, 19). Others point to the rise of conservative business factions in the Democratic Party during the 1980s. Congressman Tony Coelho, then-chair of the Democratic Congressional Campaign Committee (DCCC), actively solicited corporate money for Democratic candidates (Herrnson 2004). This development led some to conclude that business gained a voice in the Democratic Party while limiting labor's influence (Vogel 1989; Berman 1994, 117).

Some labor scholars note the Carter administration's failure to enact labor law reform and the Clinton administration's support of free trade policies as evidence of a breakdown in the relationship between labor and the Democratic Party (Brecher and Costello 1998, 31). Some point to earlier developments, such as the 1972 convention reforms in the Democratic Party, which included gender and racial quotas and primary elections as the chief means of presidential delegate selection. Many union leaders believed the reforms shut out organized labor from the process and allowed other factions in the Democratic Party to take a more prominent role in the party, at labor's expense (Battista 1991).

Unions further suffered a number of high-profile defeats on important labor legislation. In 1993, even with Democrats in control of the White House and both chambers of Congress, organized labor failed to stop passage of the North American Free Trade Agreement (NAFTA)—a bill that would remove all tariffs on over 9,000 categories of goods produced and sold in North America—despite vigorous efforts to defeat the measure. Unions also have been unable to reverse provisions of the Taft-Hartley law, which imposes a slew of restrictions on union organizing activities and grants latitude for employers to oppose organizing campaigns.

The perceived decline of organized labor has led to a lull in labor scholarship. In her summary of the literature on labor's decline, Marie Gottschalk notes that the persistent view of business as all-powerful during the 1980s created disinterest in the study of organized labor. In her words, scholars saw unions as so weak that the study of labor became tantamount to studying a "gnat harassing an elephant" (Gottschalk 2000, 37). Union political activities in particular have generally received only modest coverage in the political science literature, and less research attention in the labor literature than other aspects of unionism (see, e.g., Masters and Delaney 1987, 337).

This lack of scholarship on union political activities is problematic, given that labor's overall strength and influence throughout society is intimately tied to its political efforts. Former United Auto Workers president Walter Reuther once remarked that labor needed a strong political voice to ensure that "what the union fights for and wins at the bargaining table [cannot] be taken away in the legislative halls" (Smith 2000). The study of organized labor in American politics is thus important for several reasons.

First, unions are one of the only political vehicles for workers to express their concerns about government, and remain one of the few counters to the interests of big business. As mentioned earlier, unions provide a voice for more than sixteen million workers (with thirteen million under the umbrella of the AFL-CIO), making them one of the largest political organizations in the United States. By comparison, the powerful National Rifle Association has roughly four million members, and the Christian Coalition, which many credit for influencing the agenda of the Republican Party, has a membership of two million (National Rifle Association 2004; Christian Coalition 2004). Given that political organizations are "at the heart of the political process" (Baumgartner and Leech 1998, 188), groups with a membership total as high as the AFL-CIO and its affiliated unions certainly deserve our attention. Second, labor unions contribute to the vibrancy of democracy by mobilizing their members to participate in the political process. Unions are an outlet for workers to convey their right of expression and association, and are institutions that help workers develop the political skills necessary to become active citizens. Third, unions have been agents for social justice, and have been an important force in the passage of some of the most significant social programs in the history of the nation, including Social Security and Medicare (Greenstone 1969; Jenkins and Brents 1989; but see Quadagno 1988; Skocpol and Ikenberry 1983). Unions also serve as a moral authority for the less privileged segments of the population. Indeed, even in an era of decline, the strength and influence of unions have potentially important implications for politics, democracy, and, in the words of John Lewis, "the future of America."

Overview of the Book

Following this introduction, this book is organized into seven additional chapters. Chapter 2 addresses whether Sweeney's victory has taken organized labor in a different direction from the previous leadership of the AFL-CIO. It discusses the reasons for labor's decline in the 1970s and 1980s, and presents information about the AFL-CIO's political efforts to rebuild labor's political strength under Sweeney. Chapter 3 covers the Sweeney administration's political efforts to energize its existing membership through grassroots and political education activities. This chapter tracks changes in union members' political attitudes and beliefs, and demonstrates that labor's mobilization efforts have led to increased political participation from members of union households. It also covers how unions have responded to the obstacles of organizing more workers.

The fourth chapter discusses labor's political activities in congressional elections and weighs its efforts against those of its rivals in the business community. This chapter demonstrates that the Sweeney administration's increased commitment to grassroots and independent expenditures has helped the labor movement compete better against big business in congressional elections. The results show that labor's efforts, when weighed against business, have had a greater net effect in congressional elections in the Sweeney era than they had during the Kirkland era.

Chapter 5 examines the AFL-CIO's efforts to rely on an expanded advertising campaign during the Sweeney era. The results in this chapter demonstrate that the AFL-CIO's advertising campaign helped several Democrats win close House and Senate elections that they might otherwise have lost in the absence of the AFL-CIO's advertising campaign. Chapter 6 covers the AFL-CIO's public policy agenda. It demonstrates unions have been able to win some additional support from congressional Democrats in the Sweeney era. However, they have lost support from congressional Republicans, increasing the stakes for partisan control of Congress.

The seventh chapter speculates about organized labor's future and ends with a discussion about the implications of a stronger labor movement in the twenty-first century. The eighth and final chapter reviews the results of the 2004 election. This chapter discusses the difficult political environment that unions are likely to face with Republicans in control of the federal government. The book concludes with some thoughts on what labor must do to help Democrats regain control of the House and Senate.

Before turning to the next chapter, I wish to emphasize an important point to the reader—this is *not* a book about labor unions in the economic arena. This book does discuss labor's organizing activities in some detail in chapter 3; however, it does not specifically address issues such as strikes, workers' wages, victories in National Labor Relations Board elections, or even the "labor question," which concerns itself with the democratization of the workplace. These issues are undeniably important to the state of organized labor in the United States, but they are beyond the scope of this book. Moreover, any labor scholar would be hard-pressed to produce a study that addresses labor's organizing activities in any better systematic detail than the numerous works of Kate Bronfenbrenner and Tom Juravich. Likewise, it would be difficult to delve into issues surrounding the "labor question" in a more thoughtful manner than Nelson Lichtenstein in his book *State of the Union.*

My contribution, therefore, is to offer a book about organized labor in American politics with a specific focus on labor unions and congressional politics. The book is not a historical analysis. I discuss some historical events to add context to the book, but my analysis is largely contemporary. At the time of writing this book, John Sweeney has served as president of the AFL-CIO during four congressional election cycles—the 1996, 1998, 2000, and 2002 elections. For symmetrical comparison, I compare those elections with the four most recent elections under Lane Kirkland (the 1988, 1990, 1992, and 1994 elections). Eight elections provide a rich data set to analyze labor's campaign activities in both House and Senate elections.

The 2004 election occurred after I had already completed an initial draft of this manuscript. My subsequent revisions allowed me some additional time to make some references to the 2004 election. However, the 2004 election references came at the very late stages of this book's publication, leaving insufficient time for a systematic analysis. Instead, a descriptive account of the 2004 election is provided in the book's final chapter.

The information collected for this book comes from a variety of sources, including personal interviews with union and business leaders. The primary data for the project come from the Bureau of Labor Statistics, the Labor Research Association, Peter Hart Research Associates, the American National Election Studies, the

Federal Election Commission, the Center for Responsive Politics, and the Campaign Media Analysis Group. These diverse sources of data bring together a complete picture of labor's campaign activities, and allow for a comprehensive and systematic examination of unions and their influence in congressional elections and politics.

> We begin today to build a new AFL-CIO that will be a movement of, by, and for working Americans . . . we're going to spend whatever it takes, work as hard it takes, and stick with it as long as it takes to help American workers win the right to speak for themselves in strong unions.[1]
>
> —JOHN SWEENEY, PRESIDENT OF THE AFL-CIO

2

A Different Direction for Organized Labor?

JOHN SWEENEY VOWED to build a new labor movement when he captured the presidency of the AFL-CIO. To some observers, Sweeney's call symbolized a genuine transfer of power from organized labor's conservative elements to its more progressive wing. The Sweeney ticket, calling itself the "New Voice," conveyed in its name the clear message that it sought to represent a new direction for organized labor.

Yet debate exists over whether Sweeney and this team of "New Voice" leaders have led the labor movement in a new and different direction from that of the previous leadership of the AFL-CIO. The purpose of this chapter is to offer additional insight into this debate. It begins by discussing the changes that Sweeney has implemented since becoming president of the AFL-CIO. It covers the changes in the diversity of the AFL-CIO leadership, Sweeney's greater willingness to embrace progressive causes, and the AFL-CIO's new outreach efforts to union members. This chapter also considers some of the specific changes in organized labor's political strategies in congressional elections and the AFL-CIO's efforts to organize more workers and expand their membership.

The Changing of the Guard

John Sweeney's challenge of Lane Kirkland and later Tom Donahue was a historic break from the typical transfer of power at the AFL-CIO. Since the merger of the AFL and the CIO into one organization in 1955, there had never been a contested election for the AFL-CIO presidency. Changes in leadership were almost as uncommon. With the exception of Thomas Donahue's brief tenure as the interim president of the AFL-CIO in 1995, only two men—George Meany (1955–1979) and Lane Kirkland (1979–1995)—held the position. If fact, if one traces back in time before the merger in 1955 to the founding of the AFL in 1886, just six men—Samuel Gompers (AFL, 1886–1895; 1896–1924), John McBride (AFL, 1895), William Green (AFL, 1924–1952), John Lewis (CIO, 1935–1940), Phillip Murray (CIO, 1940–1952), and Walter Reuther (CIO, 1952–1955)—ever served as the president of the AFL or CIO. Thus, by the most generous count, since 1886 there were just nine men who preceded Sweeney as president. To put that number into perspective, there were twenty men who served as President of the United States and twenty-one men who served as Speaker of the House during the same 109-year period.

Thus, the Sweeney victory was about more than the historic challenge and overthrow of the existing leadership. The leadership change was also about transforming the labor movement. The face of the labor movement immediately became more diverse than it had been. Following Sweeney's election, fourteen women were appointed to fifty-one AFL-CIO vice president positions (AFL-CIO 1996a). Lynda Chavez-Thompson, a Hispanic woman, was appointed the organization's executive vice president. Some in the labor movement, however, contend that the AFL-CIO still lacks sufficient diversity. Leon Burris of the Postal Workers compared the challenge to the Kirkland leadership as simply "eleven white guys plotting against another group of white guys" (Moody 1996, 84). Despite that criticism, it is only fair to note that the AFL-CIO has a more diverse leadership now than at any other point in its history.

An Ideological Shift?

The rhetoric of the AFL-CIO leadership has also changed since Sweeney's election. Sweeney's predecessors, George Meany and Lane Kirkland, often went to great lengths to deny that that they were bound to traditionally liberal or conservative political positions. As Meany explained, "our goals as trade unionists are modest, for we do not seek to recast American society in any particular doctrinaire or ideological image. We seek an ever rising standard of living" (Dunlop 1990, 144). Neither Meany nor Kirkland were the first labor leaders to follow a pragmatic path. Samuel Gompers, the first president of the AFL, rejected the idea that labor unions devote their energies to broad political struggles or causes. He instead called on unions to focus on pertinent labor issues designed to produce collective goods for union members (Perlman 1928; Commons 1953; Olson 1971). Often referred to as "business unionism," this approach dominated during the Meany and Kirkland years. Sweeney and the "New Voice" leaders, however, have offered a different perspective on organized labor's purpose. Sweeney has made it a point to emphasize traditional progressive causes, notably the increasing wage and income disparities separating workers from corporate executives. The AFL-CIO's official website has a section it calls "Eye on Corporate America," which provides information on large CEO salaries and benefits.

Sweeney also began his tenure as president of the AFL-CIO with his "America Needs a Raise" campaign. Sweeney held a series of town hall meetings in which he discussed not only issues surrounding low-wage workers, but also the widespread public fears and uneasiness of the global American economy. In the spring of 1996, John Sweeney traveled to twenty cities in all regions of the nation. While George Meany often pronounced the virtues of the capitalist system as one that "rewards" both workers and investors (Buhle 1999, 91), Sweeney has not shied away from addressing the economic inequalities of capitalism (see figure 2.1).

Sweeney's willingness to appear publicly at events, such as town hall meetings, and to use the standing of his office to advance

"Answer this, Wall Street: if corporate profits are up 200 percent and executive compensation is up 400 percent, why are working family incomes down 12 percent? Answer this, corporate America: if productivity is up 24 percent and the Dow Jones is up 401 percent, why are working families running out of money, running out of credit, and running out of hope? Answer this, American government: if family values are what this election year is all about, why don't we value working families, why are moms and dads having to work three jobs just to stay even, why do workers have no time left over for their kids and their parents?

I'll answer them all: because for the past twenty years Wall Street and corporate America have been putting profits before people. Because for the past twenty years, the politicians we send to Washington have been pandering to the rich and the big corporations and pounding on the middle class and the poor. Because for the past twenty years, 97 percent of the income increase in our country has gone to the top twenty percent of wage earners. Because for the past twenty years, American workers have been worked like mules and treated like dogs, left out and shut out of decisions affecting their jobs, and because they've been fired, laid off, riffed, outsourced, temporarily replaced, permanently replaced, downsized, right-sized, marginalized, and ostracized from the very society they built with their sweat and blood. That's long enough. We've had enough. AMERICA NEEDS A RAISE!"

FIGURE 2.1 John Sweeney Speech, "America Needs a Raise Rally," June 6, 1996
Source: AFL-CIO press release, June 6, 1996, "America Needs a Raise Rally." See http://www.aflcio.org/mediacenter/prsptm/pr06061996.cfm).

labor concerns marked another departure from his predecessors. As one author explains:

> Meany and Kirkland saw themselves primarily as bureaucratic leaders, behind-the-scenes operators for a movement that didn't require their public encouragement. Sweeney conducts his share of closed door meetings, but he also sees himself as a movement leader whose

> presence symbolizes a commitment that can encourage and materially help organizers and workers embroiled in a conflict, students pondering a commitment to labor, and liberals trying to reconstruct a progressive coalition. (Meyerson 1998, 16)

Indeed, several labor scholars recognize the differences between Sweeney and his predecessors. In the words of Nelson Lichtenstein (2002, 261): "For the first time in two generations America's top trade-union leadership stood, in fact and imagination, on the left-liberal side of the nation's political culture." The philosophical and ideological differences of Sweeney compared against Meany and Kirkland are perhaps best captured by the words of a labor activist: "John Sweeney has forced unions to confront whether they'll be just be grave-diggers, or have a role in the new millenium. . . . I see people struggling with the right questions—and that's something labor hasn't seen in decades" (Meyerson 1998, 26).

Image and Outreach Efforts

A common criticism leveled against George Meany and Lane Kirkland was that neither man improved public perceptions of organized labor. Indeed, the negative public stereotype of the "big labor boss" was a common problem for George Meany. As Lloyd McBride, president of the United Steelworkers, candidly admitted in 1977, "I respect Meany greatly, but he hasn't used his office to improve our image" (U.S. News and World Report 1977, 91). Meany often took advantage of the perks of his office, handing out jobs and patronage to family members and helping himself to a chauffeured limousine, a generous expense account, and a salary that topped $100,000 (Buhle 1999, 92). As workers' wages stagnated in the 1970s, AFL-CIO leadership meetings were held at lavish resorts in Florida and the Caribbean.

Lane Kirkland fared little better in improving labor's public image. He often appeared uncomfortable on camera, avoided interviews, and lacked the commanding public presence so important in the media-driven age of the 1980s and 1990s. When Kirkland did hold press conferences, it was often to chastise the press.

Kirkland once singled out CNN political correspondent William Schneider, who had criticized Kirkland for lacking the charisma needed in the age of television politics. Indeed, even those within the labor movement recognized Kirkland's shortcomings. As one union official complained in 1995, "I am supporting Lane Kirkland, but my advice to him is, when it is called for, get in their face more" (Uchitelle 1995, 23).

By comparison, Sweeney has invested efforts into media outreach and new communications to disseminate organized labor's message. Under Sweeney, the AFL-CIO replaced the *AFL-CIO News*, an old-style newspaper, with a more colorful monthly magazine called *America@Work*, which directs its focus to encouraging social activism and promoting organized labor's public policies. Its circulation reaches between 60,000 and 75,000 top and secondary leaders, local union presidents, shop stewards, and activists. The AFL-CIO sends the magazine to the media to alert them of pressing labor issues and activities (Mort 1998).

The AFL-CIO also issues a weekly fax and e-mail, called *Work in Progress* (*WIP*), that provides information about organizing efforts, political mobilization campaigns, legislative victories, and news concerning visits or public appearances by AFL-CIO leaders. A running tally of the number of new union members reported for each week and the year to date is included at the top of the fact sheet. *WIP* also highlights brief stories about individual organizing victories from across the nation. The stories can range from organizing victories by 4,500 teachers in El Paso, Texas, to 472 workers at a potato processing plant in Blackfoot, Idaho. *WIP* serves as a central resource for chronicling organizing successes among the various local union affiliates across the full range of different professions and occupations (see, e.g., figure 2.2).

The AFL-CIO under Sweeney has thus changed its communication strategies. Its leaders are more willing to confront corporate abuses in their rhetoric and public speeches, and the AFL-CIO has also become better adept at disseminating its message through various informational sources.

New members reported in this week's WIP: 15,536
New members reported in WIP, year to date: 96,346

GOLDEN WIN FOR CAREGIVERS—A strong majority of nearly 10,000 home care workers in San Bernardino, Calif., voted for Local 434B June 6. In 1999, California unions successfully fought for a law granting organizing rights to home-care workers and requiring counties to designate an official employer for the workers. "If all home-care workers in San Bernardino get together, the system will have to listen to us," said home-care worker Wanda Bryant.

SHOW ME THE UNION—More than 4,800 workers who provide direct care to residents in state veterans' homes and mental health facilities in Missouri have a voice on the job with AFSCME, after the state's board of mediation granted the worker's desire for recognition May 30. "I don't mind working my butt off—I just want to get paid fairly for the work that I do," said Patricia Worthen, a certified nursing assistant at the Missouri Veterans Home.

ON A WIN STREAK—In a card-check campaign, 315 production, warehouse, and maintenance workers at the New Flyer Bus Company in St. Cloud, Minn., gained recognition with Communications Workers of America Local 7304 on May 11 by signing cards indicating their desire to have a union. Other workers who recently joined CWA include forty-nine production employees at KSBY-TV in San. Luis Obispo, Calif., who voted April 22 for NABET/CWA Local 59051; forty school cafeteria workers in Pennsauken, N.J., who chose Local 1034 on May 20; thirty-five employees at United Press International who for the Wire Service Guild/The Newspaper Guild/CWA May 1; and seventeen workers at Entravision-Channel 41 in Alburquerque, N.M., who are members of Local 7011.

FIGURE 2.2 Work In Progress E-Mail, June 10, 2002

Source: wip@aflcio.org.

Political Strategies in the Sweeney Era

In addition to changes in diversity, ideological perspective, and communication strategies, perhaps the most significant and sweeping changes at the AFL-CIO under John Sweeney involved its political program. In his book *America Needs a Raise*, Sweeney diagnosed several problems with labor's past political program. He writes:

> What's wrong with organized labor is similar to what's wrong with so many other organizations whose hearts are in the right place but whose minds have become complacent and whose muscles have gotten flabby. Too often, our idea of legislative and political action has degenerated into writing checks to political candidates and party organizations, lobbying entrenched members of Congress, and—shortly before Election Day—sending mailings to union members informing them of our endorsements. (Sweeney 1996, 104)

In response to this problem, Sweeney pledged to present union political information differently to its members. He explains:

> During campaigns, we [unions] should offer union members the information they need to make intelligent decisions; we should not tell them to vote for candidates because they're Democrats or because they carry the unions' endorsements. We need to become a kind of *Consumer Reports* for working families on legislative issues, public officials, and political candidates. (Sweeney 1996, 107)

There is some evidence that Sweeney has matched his words with action. Unions have spent greater sums of money on information targeted to union members. Total union expenditures on direct mail, flyers, and phone banks to union members more than doubled, from $5 million during the Kirkland era (1988–1994) to over $10 million during the Sweeney era (1996–2002), for House and Senate elections.[2] Union PACs also spent significantly more money on independent expenditures in federal elections following Sweeney's election. Independent expenditures from labor PACs increased almost six-fold from 1994 to 1996, even when adjusting for inflation (see figure 2.3). Independent expenditures from union PACs continued to grow in subsequent elections, reaching a high of more than $3.5 million in 2002. This amount was more

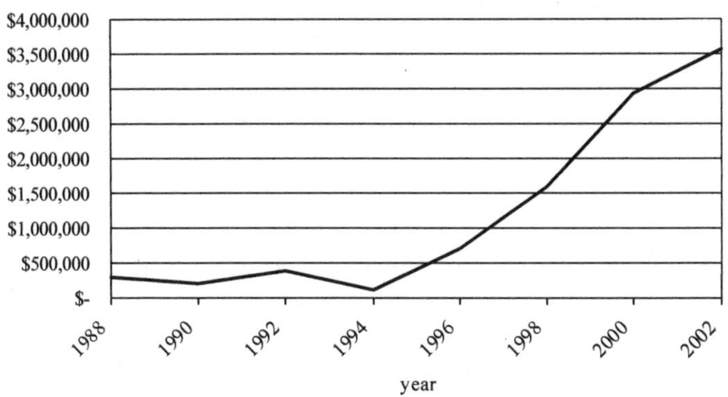

FIGURE 2.3 Independent Expenditures from Union PACs, 1988–2002

Source: Various press releases from the Federal Election Commission.

Note: All amounts are adjusted for inflation to reflect 2002 dollars.

than nine times greater (when adjusted for inflation) than what unions spent in 1992—the year in which union PACs spent the most money on independent expenditures during Lane Kirkland's tenure.

It is also worth noting that similar increases in independent expenditures from other political groups did not occur during the same time period as they did for organized labor. Independent expenditures from corporate PACs actually decreased from 1988 to 2002 when adjusting for inflation. Nonconnected PACs allocated more than $16.2 million in 1988 ($24.7 million in adjusted 2002 dollars), but spent just $2.2 million in 2002. Trade, health, and membership PACs also experienced a much smaller proportional increase in the amounts they spent on independent expenditures from 1988 to 2002 when compared to labor during the same period. In 2002 dollars, trade, health, and membership PACs spent their smallest amount on independent expenditures in 1994, when they gave $2,120,949, and they spent their largest amount in 2002, when they gave $11,589,658. This represents a five-fold increase, but one that is still significantly less than labor's twenty-eight-fold increase during the same period from 1994 to 2002. These numbers make it clear that organized labor's political assistance under Sweeney includes an increased commitment in union member communications and independent expenditures.

Partisan Political Strategies

Sweeney vowed to implement other strategic changes in labor's political program, notably to hold members of Congress accountable for antiunion positions, including those in the Democratic Party. Unions and Democrats have built a close alliance since President Franklin Roosevelt's signing of the National Industry Recovery Act of 1933, which guaranteed workers the right to bargain collectively through a representative of their choice.[3] Since the FEC began disclosing campaign contributions from PACs, unions have been one of the most partisan political contributors in congressional elections. In a typical election, Democratic candidates are the recipients of more than 90 percent of total union contributions (Gopoian 1984; Masters and Zardkoohi 1986; Saltzman 1987, 173).

Several scholars and union activists, however, have been highly critical of labor's close association with the Democratic Party, arguing that unions have received little in return for their support. Some of these critics contend that unions should consider supporting minor parties, such as the New Party or the Labor Party (Brecher and Costello 1998, 16; Buhle 1999; Slaughter 1999, 52). Others, including several union leaders, have even suggested that labor withdraw its support to Democrats who vote against labor on key issues, such as free trade (Victor 1994, 2576). Under Lane Kirkland, the AFL-CIO publicly rejected those approaches. In reference to Democrats who supported NAFTA against the strong objections of labor, Kirkland noted that the AFL-CIO does "not make judgments on the basis of a single issue; we never have. You never heard from these headquarters any suggestion that one vote on one issue is going to deter us from supporting a person whose general record on issues of concern to labor is good" (Victor 1994, 2576–2577).

Indeed, the research on labor PAC contributions suggests that unions support candidates with the strongest voting records on labor legislation (Gopoian 1984; Poole and Romer 1985; Masters and Zardkoohi 1986; Burns, Francia, and Herrnson 2000). Unions also seek to maximize their contributions by targeting their resources to prolabor candidates in competitive races (Masters and Zardkoohi 1986; Saltzman 1987, 173). In fact, unions are often more likely to consider a candidate's political vulnerability as a factor for contributing money than the member's voting record or ability to push for labor legislation (Saltzman 1987, 173). Unions further seek access with members of Congress to help shape labor legislation and contribute to powerful incumbents on influential labor committees (Grier and Munger 1986, 349).

Have these strategies changed in the Sweeney era? An examination of labor PAC campaign contributions and expenditures, as reported to the FEC, indicates that unions continue to allocate similar proportions of their funds to Democrats even after Sweeney's takeover in 1995 (see table 2.1). During the last four elections under Lane Kirkland, from 1988 to 1994, and the four elections under John Sweeney, from 1996 to 2002, union PACs gave more than 90 percent of their U.S. House contributions to Democratic candidates. Union PAC contributions to U.S. Senate candidates also went disproportionately to Democrats before and after Sweeney's election.

Of course, the strength of the two-party system in American elections is a major reason for labor's continued support of Democrats. Minor-party candidates are rarely successful in congressional elections, and withdrawing support from a viable Democratic candidate is likely to benefit Republican candidates, who typically hold more antilabor positions. As political scientist Darrell West explains: "In the eyes of labor, a bad Democrat is still going to be better than a good Republican on most issues. And it's more important for them to have [a Democrat] as Speaker" (Stevens 2002, 1). Unions thus have limited options to punish disloyal Democrats.

However, one avenue that labor has been receptive to exploring since Sweeney's election is to use the Democratic primaries

TABLE 2.1 The Partisan Distribution of Union PAC Donations to Congressional Candidates

	1988	1990	1992	1994	1996	1998	2000	2002
HOUSE								
Democrats	93%	93%	94%	95%	93%	91%	92%	90%
Republicans	7	6	5	4	6	8	8	10
Other	—	—	1	—	1	—	—	—
Total $ (thousands)	$26,789	$27,646	$30,739	$33,371	$39,638	$37,337	$43,545	$44,367
SENATE								
Democrats	92%	94%	96%	97%	94%	90%	94%	94%
Republicans	8	6	4	3	6	10	6	6
Other	—	—	—	—	—	—	—	—
Total $ (thousands)	$7,078	$5,987	$8,603	$7,279	$6,908	$6,035	$6,619	$7,534

Note: Percentages are based on union PAC donations to all House and Senate candidates running for office. Some numbers may not add to 100 percent because of rounding. A dash indicates less than 0.5 percent.

Sources: Various FEC press releases: "PAC Activity Increases for 2002 Elections," May 27, 2003; "PAC Activity Increases in 2000 Election Cycle," May 31, 2001; "FEC Releases Information on PAC Activity for 1997–98," June 8, 1999; "PAC Activity Increases in 1995–96 Election Cycle," April 22, 1997; "PAC Activity in 1994 Elections Remains at 1992 Levels," March 31, 1995; "PAC Activity Rebounds in 1991–92 Election Cycle—Unusual Nature of Contests Seen As Reason" April 29, 1993; "PAC Activity Falls in 1990 Elections," March 31, 1991; "FEC Final Report Finds Slower Growth of PAC Activity During 1988 Election Cycle," October 31, 1989.

to elect candidates who are more loyal to unions. John Pérez, the political director of the California Labor Federation, noted in an interview that there is now "more candidate accountability." He added that unions are "more likely to go after elected officials in the primary election if they are not responsive to our issues and concerns" (Pérez 2000). While it remains rare for labor to oppose a Democratic incumbent in the primary, organized labor helped orchestrate the defeats of two Democratic incumbents who supported free trade agreements.

One high-profile victory for labor occurred in the 2000 California primary, where unions helped State Senator Hilda Solis defeat nine-term Democratic incumbent Matthew Martinez by a convincing two-to-one margin (Dionne 2000). Solis served as the chair of the labor committee and killed virtually every antiunion bill in the California State Senate. Martinez, by comparison, abstained on a free trade vote involving "fast track" authority for the president in the 105th Congress. Fast track authority allows the President to negotiate trade pacts with foreign nations without Congress later altering the terms of the agreement. After abstaining from the fast track vote, Martinez indicated that he might support it in the 106th Congress. After compiling a voting record of 94 percent on labor issues in the 105th Congress, Martinez decided to support China Permanent Normal Trade Relations (PNTR) in the 106th Congress, which unions strongly opposed. Despite Martinez's strong overall voting record on labor issues, his support of free trade positions in the 106th Congress outweighed his support for other labor issues. Miguel Contreras, the executive-treasurer of the Los Angeles County Federation of Labor, explained, "We're sending a message. This is a very blue-collar, union district. We ought to be sending warriors from these districts and not just someone who'll give us a vote occasionally. . . . Marty was not terrible. . . . But we're looking for 100 percent" (Dionne 2000). Pérez added, "Hilda is simply a more responsive legislator than Marty. We're willing to go into more primaries and make a difference. That's the direction we're going to take" (Pérez 2000).

In 2002, unions scored a similar victory when they supported Ohio State Senator Tim Ryan against incumbent Tom Sawyer, who had supported numerous free trade bills (including NAFTA, fast track, and China PNTR) while serving in Congress. Redistricting in 2002 altered Sawyer's constituency to one that included the city of Youngstown and its large number of unemployed steel workers, who opposed the free trade agreements that Sawyer had supported. Ryan, on the other hand, made opposition to free trade one of the hallmarks of his campaign. The strong support Ryan received from several unions helped him score a surprising and impressive seventeen-point victory over Sawyer. Sawyer conceded that unions played a large role in his defeat. "I would submit that steel probably has been genuinely hurt by fair trade practices. It's true that steelworkers were angry and scared and that had a very real effect on the race" (Stevens 2002, 1).

Of course, the Solis and Ryan victories are anecdotes, and do not demonstrate any broad shift in labor's political strategies. Still, both races are instructive of how unions have become willing, when the right conditions present themselves, to hold Democrats accountable. While the old leadership of the AFL-CIO publicly rejected making "judgments on the basis of a single issue," several unions have become more willing in the Sweeney era to punish Democrats who support free trade or other antiunion policies.

Targeting Competitive Races

One of the overriding goals in organized labor's support of Democratic candidates has been to help the Democratic Party regain control of Congress. To maximize the number of seats that Democrats win, organized labor must direct its resources (which include direct contributions, in-kind contributions, independent expenditures, communication expenditures, and other miscellaneous expenditures) to the most competitive elections. Since Sweeney's election, the AFL-CIO has led this effort to most effectively target resources. As the results in table 2.2 indicate, the AFL-CIO targeted a significantly greater percentage of its resources into competitive House and Senate elections under the Sweeney leadership than it had under the Kirkland leadership. When examining the funds allocated to House incumbents seeking reelection, the

TABLE 2.2 The Distribution of AFL-CIO Contributions and Expenditures in Competitive Races

	KIRKLAND (1988–1994)	SWEENEY (1996–2002)
HOUSE		
Incumbents		
Competitive	48%	61%
Uncompetitive	52	39
Total $ (in thousands)	$4,373	$4,681
Challengers		
Competitive	64%	86%
Uncompetitive	36	14
Total $ (in thousands)	$1,451	$4,212
Open seats		
Competitive	73%	87%
Uncompetitive	27	13
Total $ (in thousands)	$1,610	$3,349
SENATE		
Incumbents		
Competitive	61%	88%
Uncompetitive	39	12
Total $ (in thousands)	$2,180	$3,304
Challengers		
Competitive	71%	91%
Uncompetitive	29	9
Total $ (in thousands)	$1,296	$1,607
Open seats		
Competitive	86%	90%
Uncompetitive	14	10
Total $ (in thousands)	$1,016	$3,011

Note: Percentages are based on AFL-CIO PAC contributions and expenditures to general election House and Senate candidates. This includes all direct contributions, in-kind contributions, independent expenditures, communication expenditures, and other miscellaneous expenditures on behalf of the candidate. Independent and communication expenditures against a candidate's opponent are also treated as expenditures on behalf of the candidate. A "competitive" contest is defined as a race decided by 0 to 20 points; an "uncompetitive" contest is defined as a race decided by 21 points or more. Dollar amounts are indexed for inflation to reflect 2002 dollars.

results show that during the Kirkland period, the AFL-CIO spent 48 percent of its PAC contributions and expenditures in competitive races, with the remaining 52 percent going to incumbents in uncompetitive contests. By comparison, the AFL-CIO, during the Sweeney period, targeted 61 percent of its PAC contributions and expenditures to House incumbents in competitive races with only 39 percent going to incumbents in uncompetitive contests.

The differences between the Kirkland and Sweeney periods are even starker when examining elections involving House challengers and open-seat candidates. During the Kirkland period, 64 percent of the AFL-CIO's campaign funds spent on House challengers went to those in competitive races, compared to 86 percent during the Sweeney period. Of the money spent on House open-seat candidates, 73 percent of the AFL-CIO's contributions and expenditures went to those in competitive races during the Kirkland period, compared to 87 percent during the Sweeney period. Similar patterns were also present in Senate elections. Competitive Senate incumbents, challengers, and open-seat candidates all received a greater share of the AFL-CIO's contributions and expenditures in the Sweeney period than they did during the Kirkland period.

These results make clear that the AFL-CIO has altered its contribution strategies under the Sweeney leadership, with a significantly greater portion of its funds now being spent in competitive contests. This shift in strategy was at least partly due to the Republican takeover of Congress following the 1994 election. The AFL-CIO needed to alter the composition of Congress after the Republican takeover. This required shifting resources to more competitive races, to help vulnerable Democratic incumbents remain in power and to assist promising Democratic challengers and open-seat candidates who had an opportunity to win Republican-held seats. With Democrats in the minority for the first time in four decades, the AFL-CIO had to rely more on electoral or ideological strategies and less on access strategies, in which money flows to powerful incumbents who may face only token opposition in their elections.

While the change in power that followed the 1994 election dictated that new political strategies were in order, the AFL-CIO could have fallen into the trap of responding and reacting too slowly to the new political circumstances on Capitol Hill. This, however, was not the case. As the results demonstrate, the Sweeney leadership responded effectively to the Republican takeover of Congress by wasting very few resources in uncompetitive elections.

Following the Lead of the AFL-CIO

The activities of the AFL-CIO alone constitute only a fraction of organized labor's overall political efforts. The more important question is whether the labor community as a whole followed the lead of the AFL-CIO by directing its resources into competitive congressional contests. The numbers in table 2.3 confirm that this was indeed the case.

From 1988 to 1994, unions contributed and spent nearly $20.1 million (in 2002 dollars) on House challengers who competed in the general election (see table 2.3). Of that amount, 66 percent went to challengers in competitive races. By comparison, unions contributed and spent nearly $29.5 million on challengers from 1996 to 2002 and devoted 81 percent of that money to challengers in competitive races.

Likewise, union contributions and expenditures have been better targeted in House open-seat contests. During the Kirkland period, unions contributed and spent 71 percent of their resources on competitive contests. However, during the Sweeney period, unions targeted 84 percent of their resources on competitive races.

Among House incumbents, unions contributed and spent more money on safe incumbents than on vulnerable incumbents. During the Kirkland period, unions contributed and spent almost $109 million (in 2002 dollars) on House incumbents, giving 60 percent to those in safe races. During the Sweeney period, unions contributed and spent roughly $89 million on House incumbents. Of that amount, 67 percent went to safe incumbents. Thus, despite

TABLE 2.3 The Distribution of Union Contributions and Expenditures in Competitive Races

	KIRKLAND (1988–1994)	SWEENEY (1996–2002)
HOUSE		
Incumbents		
Competitive	40%	33%
Uncompetitive	60	67
Total $ (in thousands)	$108,712	$89,347
Challengers		
Competitive	66%	81%
Uncompetitive	34	19
Total $ (in thousands)	$20,098	$29,471
Open seats		
Competitive	71%	84%
Uncompetitive	29	16
Total $ (in thousands)	$21,655	$21,226
SENATE		
Incumbents		
Competitive	58%	60%
Uncompetitive	42	40
Total $ (in thousands)	$20,327	$14,423
Challengers		
Competitive	77%	83%
Uncompetitive	23	17
Total $ (in thousands)	$10,734	$7,507
Open seats		
Competitive	84%	90%
Uncompetitive	16	10
Total $ (in thousands)	$6,995	$10,294

Note: Percentages are based on all labor PAC contributions and expenditures to general election House and Senate candidates. This includes all direct contributions, in-kind contributions, independent expenditures, communication expenditures, and other miscellaneous expenditures on behalf of the candidate. Independent and communication expenditures against a candidate's opponent are also treated as expenditures on behalf of the candidate. A "competitive" contest is defined as a race decided by 0 to 20 points; an "uncompetitive" contest is defined as a race decided by 21 points or more. Dollar amounts are indexed for inflation to reflect 2002 dollars.

the AFL-CIO's greater investment in competitive incumbents, the labor community as a whole continued to invest in safe incumbents, presumably to maintain access to those likely to remain in office. This mixed strategy suggests that the labor movement as a whole has been somewhat less aggressive in responding to the Republican takeover of Congress than the AFL-CIO.

Many of these patterns were also consistent in the U.S. Senate. Safe and vulnerable Senate incumbents received almost identical proportions of money from union PACs during the Sweeney period as they did during the Kirkland period. However, union PACs again were able to target a greater percentage of their resources into competitive races for Senate challengers and open-seat candidates. Unions contributed and spent 83 percent of their resources in competitive Senate races during the Sweeney years, compared to 77 percent during the Kirkland years. Likewise, in open-seat Senate races, unions contributed and spent 90 percent of their resources in competitive Senate races during the Sweeney years, compared to 84 percent during the Kirkland period.

Taken together, these results suggest that unions targeted their resources more efficiently in the Sweeney era than they did in the Kirkland era. The AFL-CIO led by example, spending fewer dollars in uncompetitive elections during the Sweeney period than it did in the Kirkland period. Overall, unions have followed the lead of the AFL-CIO, allocating a smaller proportion of their money on uncompetitive challengers and open-seat candidates during the Sweeney era than they did during the Kirkland era.

Organizing the Unorganized

In addition to changes in the AFL-CIO's political strategies, the cornerstone of John Sweeney's "New Voice" platform was to increase organized labor's efforts and resources to organize more workers. Organizing workers has important political implications worth stressing. The more workers that unions can add to its ranks, the more influence they are likely to wield in the political and legislative process.

Upon taking office, Sweeney pledged to organize workers at an "unprecedented pace and scale" (Bronfenbrenner and Juravich 1998, 19). In his first year in office, Sweeney promised to spend \$20 million on organizing (Swoboda 1995b). He also pledged another \$60 million for a public relations campaign to improve labor's image and create a more formidable climate for organizing (Greenhouse 1997). As Sweeney explained shortly after becoming president of the AFL-CIO: "The most important thing we can do, starting right now today, is to organize every working woman and man who needs a better deal and a new voice. As long as we speak for scarcely one-sixth of the work force, we will never be able to win what we deserve at the bargaining table or in the legislative process" (Greenhouse 1995).

Sweeney's aggressive steps were in response to the lack of attention that previous leadership had paid to organizing. During most of the Meany administration, the percentage of union members in the workforce dropped steadily. Yet Meany's response to this decline was indifference. As he stated to a reporter in the 1970s, "Why should we worry about organizing groups of people who do not appear to want to be organized?" (Perl 1987). Meany's successor, Lane Kirkland, took the issue more seriously, creating the AFL-CIO's Organizing Institute, which trains new organizers and activists involved in organizing campaigns. However, he viewed organizing largely to be a matter for local unions to address, and many of his own comments sounded similar to Meany's. In 1992, Kirkland told reporters, "We are here to organize all workers *who want a voice*" (italics added, Butterfield 1992). According to Michael Goldfield (1987, 226), union organizing efforts in the 1980s had "become less aggressive and, in general, less committed to new organizing campaigns in the private sector."

Both Meany and Kirkland failed to make any significant allocations of the AFL-CIO's resources toward organizing. During both the Meany and Kirkland years, real expenditures on organizing per nonunion member steadily decreased (Goldfield 1986, 24). Expenditures on organizing activities, which were roughly 40 percent of the AFL and CIO operating budgets in the 1940s and 1950s, had become almost nonexistent by 1995 (Kosterlitz 1999, 2472).

Sweeney, by contrast, viewed organizing as a key to labor's revitalization. Sweeney (1996, 86) explains:

> The decline in organizing meant that unions had virtually stopped conducting a dialogue with working Americans outside our ranks. One of many reasons that organizing is an essential element of unionism is that it keeps us abreast with the aspirations, attitudes, and conditions of working people beyond our own workplaces—information that's essential for us in representing our own members as well as in expanding our membership base.

Shortly after winning office, Sweeney created a new Organizing Department to assist unions in their organizing efforts and to oversee the Organizing Institute. The Organizing Department was initially headed by Richard Bensinger, who, in one author's words, "became a roving apostle of organizing to internationals and central labor councils" (Meyerson 1998, 16). In 1998, Sweeney replaced Bensinger with Kirk Adams, a former Service Employees International Union (SEIU) organizer, who continued to stress the importance of organizing.

The AFL-CIO executive council provided strong financial backing for its Organizing Department, significantly increasing money for its organizing fund. Several local unions also followed the AFL-CIO's lead. In less than two years after Sweeney's election, the number of local unions that devoted 10 to 20 percent of their resources into organizing new workers increased from 15 to 150 (Bensinger 1998). The Hotel and Restaurant Employees (HERE, which became UNITE HERE in 2004), in particular, has been a model for organizing. In Las Vegas alone, it organized more than 45,000 hotel workers. Likewise, the SEIU, under the leadership of Andrew Stern, allocates 47 percent of its budget to organizing, and nearly all the local affiliates of the SEIU spend at least 20 percent of their resources on organizing (Bensinger 1998).

Another significant difference between the Sweeney leadership and his predecessors is on the issue of illegal immigration. Under Sweeney, the AFL-CIO executive board voted in February 2000 to support amnesty for an estimated 6 million illegal immigrants and to end employer sanctions against companies that hire them. In a released statement, the AFL-CIO announced, "We strongly believe employer sanctions, as a nationwide policy applied to all workplaces, has failed and should be eliminated. It should be replaced with an alternative policy to reduce undocumented immigration and prevent employer abuse" (AFL-CIO 2000a). Ironically, the sanctions were enacted into law at the urging of the AFL-CIO just fifteen years earlier. Unions have changed their position on illegal immigration in an effort to build closer ties with immigrant workers.

Organized labor had previously stood against open immigration policies because union leaders believed that immigrant workers would bring competition to the labor market, driving wages down and making it more difficult for unemployed workers to find jobs. Moreover, unions considered immigrant workers to be difficult to organize because immigrants often fear deportation (Moody 1997, 163). However, several of the most successful organizing campaigns in the 1990s involved immigrant workers (Delgado 1993). Latino immigrants in southern California, for example, led the "Justice for Janitors" campaign and won a contract from a major building cleaning contractor that increased union membership in the Local 399 union from 1,800 to 8,000. This successful campaign represented the largest private sector union victory since the efforts of United Farm Workers in the 1970s (Milkman and Wong 2001, 100).

In addition to the AFL-CIO's increased organizing budget and its effort to organize immigrant workers, union affiliates have engaged in new techniques designed to circumvent the NLRB process (see Goldfield 1987, 86–87 for an excellent summary of this process). Many unions now attempt to organize workers through so-called "bargaining to organize" strategies. The most common of these new strategies is "card-check" neutrality agreements. The card-check process is a voluntary agreement in which employers agree to stay "neutral" and not wage antiunion campaigns when a majority of workers sign union cards. Employers submit to the card-check agreements often because unions have gained leverage over the company and apply pressure (Sherman and Voss 2000,

86). This method of union recognition avoids the long delays that have become commonplace in the NLRB process.

Unions often put pressure on companies to accept neutrality agreements through a second method called the "corporate campaign." In a typical corporate campaign, union researchers uncover unflattering (or in some cases illegal) activities by companies and their officials. The union may bring this information to the attention of the media or an interest group to generate public backlash against the company, which in turn builds pressure on the company to yield to the union's demands. Sweeney has endorsed local affiliates to engage in corporate campaigns. In his words, "Labor must organize without the law so that we can later organize under the law" (Lichtenstein 1999, 106). Sweeney also created the Center for Strategic Campaigns and the Worker Ownership and Governance Institute to assist corporate campaign efforts (AFL-CIO 1996b). These actions represent a break from his predecessors, who typically frowned on untraditional organizing methods that went beyond the NLRB process.

Sweeney also initiated Union Summer in 1996. The program actively recruited college students to organize workers throughout the nation. In just the first two months of the program, college interns delivered more than 150,000 prounion leaflets and helped organize roughly 235 protests and rallies for workers across the United States (AFL-CIO 1996a). The alliance of labor and college students marked yet another departure from the policies of Sweeney's predecessors. In 1969, for example, AFL-CIO president George Meany instructed his staff to monitor "student troublemakers" in the Students for a Democratic Society, who attempted to win sympathy for unions and its workers with a planned summer "work-in" (Buhle 1999, 258).

But perhaps the most significant change between Sweeney and his predecessors with respect to organizing is in attitude. As one former union official who worked for Lane Kirkland explained, "During Kirkland's presidency, we were intellectually convinced—because of the law, because of the economy—that organizing was impossible. The people around Sweeney believe they can organize" (Bensinger 1998). The AFL-CIO's more aggressive actions produced some early results. Organizing campaigns were able to unionize 373,000 new members in 1998. The union ranks increased by 100,000 after accounting for job losses and layoffs. The number of union certification elections increased 8.9 percent from 1997 to 1998. The elections were also slightly more successful. Unions won 51.7 percent of elections in 1998 compared to 49.2 percent in 1997 (AFL-CIO 1999a). The numbers improved further in 1999. Unions recruited 600,000 new members, for a net gain of 265,000. This included 112,000 in the private sector, marking the largest growth in more than two decades (Greenhouse 2000a).

Despite these early trends, later figures have been less encouraging. Union density fell from 13.9 percent in 1999 to 13.5 percent in 2000, 13.4 percent in 2001, and 13.2 percent in 2002 (see figure 2.4). Lipset and Katchanovski (2001, 242) conclude from these numbers that the "efforts of the Sweeney-led administration of the AFL-CIO have had little effect." There also have been some notable organizing failures during Sweeney's tenure. The AFL-CIO spent a reported $90,000 per month to assist the United Farm Workers in organizing strawberry pickers in California. The AFL-CIO recruited civil rights, feminist, and environmental activists to aid the cause. Despite the high-profile campaign, the AFL-CIO was able to organize just 750 workers out of 20,000 potential recruits (Judis 2001). The AFL-CIO also spent $1.2 million on the Building Trades Organizing Project to organize 60,000 construction workers in Las Vegas. One member of the project dubbed it "the largest organizing campaign ever to be launched in the labor movement" (Judis 2001). Yet within three years the project failed to make any significant progress and folded.

Perhaps the largest loss under Sweeney's tenure was the exit of the 500,000-member United Brotherhood of Carpenters from the AFL-CIO in 2001. Most stinging of all is that the Carpenters' stated reason for leaving the AFL-CIO was that Sweeney had not been aggressive enough in organizing more workers. President of the Carpenters Douglas McCarron issued a rebuke of Sweeney upon announcing his union's withdrawal, stating:

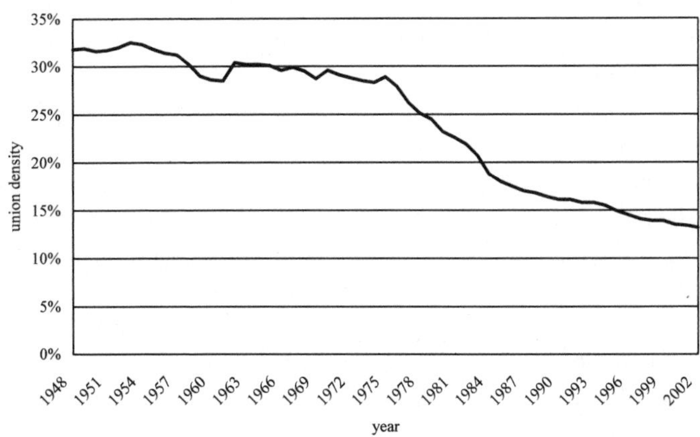

FIGURE 2.4 Union Membership as a Proportion of the Labor Force
Source: Labor Research Association; Bureau of Labor Statistics.

> The union has reorganized in the last few years to shift resources to organizing and had hoped the AFL-CIO would make similar changes. After five years, I have seen nothing to indicate the AFL-CIO is seriously considering changes that would cure these problems, nor do I see any realistic chance that an investment of more time or resources by the UBC will alter those facts. (McCarron 2001)

Despite McCarron's charge, information obtained from AFL-CIO Executive Council Reports indicates that the AFL-CIO spent considerably more money on organizing since 1995, when Sweeney became president (see table 2.4). Organizing expenditures under Kirkland were virtually nonexistent from 1987 to 1994, totaling one percent or less of the AFL-CIO budget in each of those years. In 1995, just before Sweeney's takeover, the AFL-CIO began to increase its expenditures on organizing, spending roughly $2.7 million. By 1996, Sweeney's first full year as president, the AFL-CIO significantly increased its spending on organizing campaigns, allocating $8.4 million—a three-fold increase from the previous year. The amounts spent on organizing increased in each successive year, with $14 million allocated in 1997, $15.3 million allocated in 1998, $15.8 million allocated in 1999, and $15.9 million in 2000.

These budget allocations demonstrate that organizing campaigns have received much greater financial backing under Sweeney than in the past. Moreover, the Sweeney leadership deserves some credit for reversing the previous leadership's almost complete lack of attention and commitment to organizing efforts. However, the continued decline in union density suggests that the AFL-CIO will need to commit even more resources to organizing more workers.

Indeed, the amount of money needed to make a significant difference in union density is daunting. Unions need to add about 300,000 new members a year just to maintain their current density. For unionization to reach 30 percent of the workforce, unions will need to organize at least twenty-five million more workers. The average cost to organize a single worker is $1,000, meaning that the total cost to reach the 30 percent level would cost unions a staggering $25 billion (Kaden, Keilin, O'Cleireacain, and Simon 1999, 37). While the AFL-CIO certainly cannot afford $25 billion, the huge costs associated with making a significant difference in union density underscore the need for the AFL-CIO to commit even more resources than it presently does to organizing.

Of course, money and resources are only part of the solution to organizing more workers. Current labor laws are a major obstacle. The Taft-Hartley Act of 1947, for example, prohibits secondary boycotts and mass picketing, and allows states the right to pass "right-to-work" laws, which prohibit union membership as a condition of employment. Right-to-work laws exist in twenty-one states. Employers are also allowed under the law to hire permanent replacements for striking workers and to run antiunion campaigns directed at its workers. Unions have long fought to have this law overturned, arguing that it undercuts their bargaining power and leverage with employers. In addition to the Taft-Hartley Act, the Landrum-Griffin Act of 1959 reduced labor's ability to pressure employers. The law banned "hot cargo" agreements—a practice

TABLE 2.4 AFL-CIO Expenses, 1987–2000

	1987	1988	1989	1990	1991	1992	1993	1994	1995	1996	1997	1998	1999	2000
Organizing	$154	$14	$169	$60	$115	$48	$48	$30	$2,678	$8,419	$14,057	$15,330	$15,847	$15,870
	1%	0%	1%	0%	1%	0%	0%	0%	5%	9%	17%	15%	20%	14%
Field services and mobilization	$1,869	$2,218	$2,568	$3,108	$2,777	$2,649	$2,295	$2,202	$12,530	$13,915	$27,577	$45,924	$26,629	$57,468
	10%	10%	13%	12%	12%	10%	10%	8%	23%	14%	34%	46%	34%	51%
Political expenses	$5,304	$8,239	$5,470	$8,862	$5,748	$9,236	$6,497	$10,256	$6,824	$46,999	$4,119	$5,454	$2,886	$3,294
	28%	37%	27%	35%	25%	35%	28%	39%	12%	48%	5%	5%	4%	3%
Education and information	$3,705	$3,288	$3,526	$3,145	$3,345	$3,262	$3,330	$3,380	$5,113	$5,125	$1,064	$1,104	$1,014	$909
	19%	15%	17%	12%	15%	12%	14%	13%	9%	5%	1%	1%	1%	1%
International affairs	$1,480	$1,741	$1,649	$1,908	$2,140	$2,141	$2,102	$1,867	$5,403	$5,098	$2,460	$2,463	$2,691	$2,705
	8%	8%	8%	8%	9%	8%	9%	7%	10%	5%	3%	2%	3%	2%
Public policy and legislation	$1,590	$1,635	$1,728	$1,898	$2,219	$2,098	$2,007	$2,009	$5,872	$5,407	$3,834	$4,272	$4,469	$4,657
	8%	7%	8%	8%	10%	8%	9%	8%	11%	6%	5%	4%	6%	4%

continued

TABLE 2.4 AFL-CIO Expenses, 1987–2000 (*continued*)

	1987	1988	1989	1990	1991	1992	1993	1994	1995	1996	1997	1998	1999	2000
Occupational safety and health	$1,047	$1,021	$1,090	$521	$519	$571	$619	$707	$702	$694	$728	$631	$788	$807
	5%	5%	5%	2%	2%	2%	3%	3%	1%	1%	1%	1%	1%	1%
Civil/human rights and working women	$518	$495	$496	$471	$500	$576	$607	$636	$647	$960	$1,344	$1,653	$1,680	$1,874
	3%	2%	2%	2%	2%	2%	3%	2%	1%	1%	2%	2%	2%	2%
Corporate and public affairs	$1,629	$1,684	$1,661	$1,786	$1,864	$2,073	$2,233	$2,289	$6,189	$6,721	$7,640	$7,959	$9,786	$9,976
	9%	8%	8%	7%	8%	8%	10%	9%	11%	7%	9%	8%	13%	9%
Other expenses	$1,836	$2,007	$2,087	$3,539	$3,824	$3,745	$3,373	$3,061	$8,701	$4,113	$18,154	$15,439	$12,466	$14,310
	10%	9%	10%	14%	17%	14%	15%	12%	16%	4%	22%	15%	16%	13%

Source: AFL-CIO Executive Council Reports (1989, 1991, 1993, 1995, 1997, 1999, 2001).

Note: Dollar amounts are in thousands of dollars.

in which one company refuses to handle the products of another company involved in a labor dispute.

Employer tactics have also thwarted organizing efforts. Corporations and businesses have waged more intense antiunion campaigns over time, relying on methods that include firing workers for engaging in organizing activities, holding one-on-one supervisor meetings with employees, and distributing antiunion letters and leaflets (Goldfield 1987, 51; Bronfenbrenner and Juravich 1998, 28). One study found that from 1960 to 1980, there was a threefold increase in the firing of workers for union activity (Freeman 1985, 53). Another study reported that roughly one in twenty workers who voted for a union were illegally discharged (Goldfield 1986, 10). Federal law also permits employers to campaign against union organizing efforts in the workplace, but prohibits union organizers from the company premises. Union certification elections are held at the workplace, allowing employers to continue any antiunion campaigning right up until the very moment that workers enter the polls to cast their ballots. Union organizers, on the other hand, have no such luxury.

Even when unions win NLRB elections to represent workers, companies will often challenge the result, delaying contract negotiations for years. In other instances, companies recognize the union but then fail to bargain in good faith, often leading to an impasse in the negotiations and ultimately a "lockout," which prevents workers from returning to the job until a collective bargaining agreement is reached (Sweeney 1996, 82). Businesses have even stepped up their efforts to decertify existing unions (Freeman and Medoff 1984).

Population shifts to southern and southwestern states are another development that has posed a challenge to organizing efforts. Organizing has been less successful in these regions (Kearney 1982; Goldfield 1987). Union density is 6 percent or less of the workforce in southern states such as Arkansas, Mississippi, North Carolina, South Carolina, Texas, and Virginia. By comparison, union workers make up 20 percent or more of the workforce in northern states, such as Michigan, New Jersey, and New York (Bureau of Labor Statistics 2005). Some contend that the reason for labor's failure to unionize workers in the Sunbelt and the South is a function of the region's culture and unfavorable legal climate to organizing campaigns (Kearney 1992, 32–34).

Despite these numerous obstacles, the labor movement may be able to rebuild itself, and more quickly than some might imagine. Union growth often occurs in "spurts." Indeed, "spurt theory" suggests that unionization of the workforce has historically expanded in short periodic bursts after years of stagnation, rather than through steady growth (Freeman 1986). The rapid rise of the CIO in the 1930s and 1940s and the growth of the AFL in the early 1900s are two examples that support spurt theory. Although there are no indications that any spurt in union density is likely to occur in the near future, the labor movement has confronted similar membership crises in the past and has been able to rebound. For this reason alone, organized labor must remain vigilant in its organizing efforts. If unions can begin to succeed in these efforts and build sizable memberships in congressional districts, organized labor could exert more constituent pressures on members of Congress.

Summary

The changes that have occurred at the AFL-CIO since 1996 suggest that labor has undergone a number of significant changes. First, Sweeney's AFL-CIO is more diverse and has altered its communications strategies. Second, Sweeney's AFL-CIO has made significant changes in its political program. While unions have remained steadfast supporters of Democratic congressional candidates, labor has begun to use the Democratic primary to defeat a few incumbents, mainly for their support of free trade policies. This suggests that unions can and will hold some elected officials accountable for antiunion positions. Third, Sweeney's AFL-CIO has allocated more of its resources into competitive congressional races than in the past. This has meant that fewer resources have been spent on challengers and open-seat candidates who were likely to lose, and more money has gone into assisting nonincumbents in competitive races. The AFL-CIO has even been aggressive in races involving incumbents, with the bulk of money again going to those in the most competitive races. The AFL-CIO appears to have adopted a very clear electoral strategy designed to help Democrats regain majority control of Congress. The AFL-CIO has also taken other aggressive steps to rebuild labor's political power. Perhaps most important, Sweeney's AFL-CIO has expanded labor's political activities to include an increased investment on independent expenditures and internal communications to mobilize its membership.

Finally, the Sweeney leadership has been more aggressive in combating labor's membership decline. While the results have been less than encouraging, Sweeney deserves credit for recognizing the severity of the problem and for using the powers of his office to allocate more money to organizing efforts. The AFL-CIO, however, will need to spend more money on organizing and consider even bolder initiatives to address this continuing problem.

In summary, Sweeney's AFL-CIO is not a shell of the old. The words and actions of the new AFL-CIO leadership are quite different from those of their predecessors. Nevertheless, changes must also bring results. What effects have the AFL-CIO's reforms had on union members? Have they had an effect on congressional elections and policy? I turn to these important questions in the chapters that follow.

We've never seen such excitement and such entrhusiasm from rank-and-file workers. They're truly engaged.[1]

—GERALD MCENTEE, PRESIDENT OF THE AMERICAN FEDERATION OF STATE, COUNTY, ANF MUNICIPAL EMPLOYEES

3

Strength in Numbers

Organizing and Mobilizing Union Members

UNIONS, PERHAPS AS much as any political organization, depend on their members for their political strength (Schlozman and Tierney 1986, 105). A mobilized membership can translate into a greater number of voters and activists for organized labor, and increases its pool for financial contributions (Masters and Delaney 1987). One study concluded that labor's manpower has a greater effect on elections than its endorsements or campaign contributions (Bok and Dunlop 1970). As one labor official explains, "Money is important, but if you haven't got the grassroots base, you ain't got it" (Gerber 1999, 83). As noted earlier, however, unions experienced precipitous declines in membership as a percentage of the American workforce over the last fifty years, with the losses becoming more pronounced over the last quarter of a century.

In addition to the erosion of its membership, unions often failed to mobilize and deliver a substantial percentage of union voters to Democratic candidates throughout much of the 1980s and early 1990s. Former House Speaker Newt Gingrich, a frequent union critic, seized on statistics that indicated more than two out of every five union workers voted for Republican candidates, often in conflict with the AFL-CIO's endorsements. He attacked unions for "coercing" members into having their own funds used to support a disproportionate number of Democrats when a large number of union members supported Republicans (Nelson 1996).

As stressed in the previous chapter, one of John Sweeney's priorities upon assuming the presidency of the AFL-CIO was to organize more workers and to commit significant union resources toward education efforts and political mobilization of its existing membership. Yet organizing union members has become a serious challenge over the past several decades, as manufacturing and industrial companies, which once provided a stable occupation and a livable wage for low-skilled workers, began a steady and gradual exodus from the United States to countries with a low-wage workforce (Lichtenstein 2002). Once a militant force in the labor movement, industrial and manufacturing unions, rather than working to expand their base, have been forced to focus on protecting the union jobs remaining in the United States. Moreover, industrial and manufacturing workers have historically been among the most politically active members of the labor movement, presenting a challenge to labor's political mobilization efforts. Thus, upon taking office, Sweeney faced several significant obstacles in his efforts to organize and mobilize union members.

This chapter begins by providing an overview of how the union workforce has evolved over the past century and discusses how these changes present both difficulties and opportunities for the future of the labor movement. The chapter then shifts to considering the effect of Sweeney's reforms on the political attitudes and behavior of union members. Have union members' political behavior and attitudes changed, and have union members become more politically active since Sweeney's election?

Changes in the Union Workforce

During the height of union density in the mid-1950s, union members largely consisted of workers in the manufacturing sector. However, as figure 3.1 indicates, there have been significant

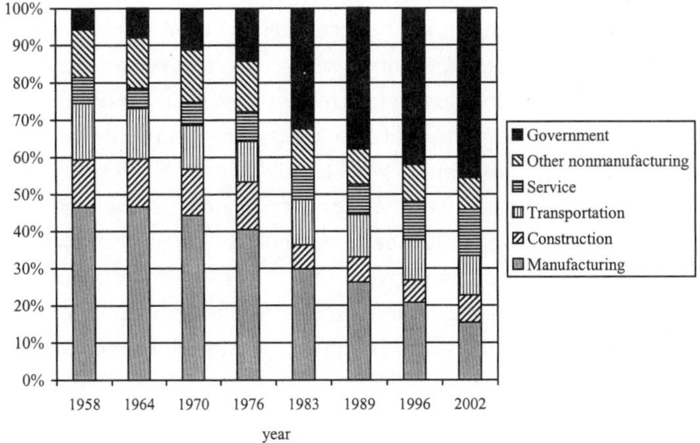

FIGURE 3.1 Union Members by Industry

Source: The U.S. Bureau of Labor Statistics.

changes in the occupational composition of the union workforce over the past several decades. In 1956, almost half of the union workforce held jobs in the manufacturing sector. This percentage fell to 30 percent in the mid-1980s, and then to less than 20 percent by 2000.

The erosion of the American manufacturing sector has forced unions to begin organizing workers in other sectors of the economy. Government and public sector workers, including public school teachers, have largely filled the void created by manufacturing losses. The American Federation of Teachers (AFT) and the National Education Association (NEA) comprise more than 3.5 million members combined.[2] The largest and most influential union in the public sector is American Federation of State, County, and Municipal Employees. AFSCME's membership has grown from slightly more than 250,000 members in the mid-1960s to some 1.4 million members in 2003.

In addition to the strength of individual unions, such as the NEA, AFT, and AFSCME, the overall shift in union membership to the public sector has been quite dramatic over the past half century. In the mid-1950s, just one of every twenty union workers held a job in the government or public sector. By the 1980s, however, public sector workers represented more than one-third of all union members. By the beginning of the twenty-first century, more than two out of every five union workers held jobs in the public sector. One reason for this large increase can be traced back to 1961, when President John F. Kennedy passed Executive Order 10988. The law allows public employees the right to bargain collectively on nonwage issues in the federal sector. Additionally, public sector workers were less difficult to organize, because they had formerly belonged to employee associations. These associations were ultimately transformed into unions (Johnston 2001, 44).

The growth of public sector unionism is also a product of organized labor's higher success rates in winning union certification elections for public sector workers. Indeed, public sector workers vote for union representation in more than 80 percent of certification elections, compared to just 48 percent in the private sector. This substantial difference is explained in part by the fact that employers are less likely in the public sector than the private sector to oppose organizing campaigns (Juravich and Bronfenbrenner 1998, 262–282).

The growth of unions in the public sector has prompted economist Leo Troy to refer to the development as the "New Unionism." Troy notes that union members in the public sector now exceed the size of the CIO at its peak and the membership of the old AFL throughout most of its years (Troy 1994, 158). He predicts new unionism will become "the center of union power" in the United States. Indeed, some could argue that the public sector unions already are the center of union power. For example, some political pundits have described Gerald McEntee, the president of AFSCME, as a "kingmaker" in national Democratic Party politics (Will 2003).

While the public sector has been the major area for union growth, there also have been some gains in the service sector. Low-skilled workers once dominated the manufacturing sector, but these workers now often find their work in the service sector as janitors, waiters, or dishwashers. The Service Employees International Union has taken aggressive steps to organize this sector of the economy, spending almost half its budget on organizing activities. The SEIU increased its membership at a rate of 70,000 to 80,000 in 2000, marking a significant increase from its rate of 20,000 to 30,000 per year in the mid-1990s (Stern 2001, 23; Greenhouse 2000a).

Low-skilled blue-collar workers, however, no longer constitute a majority of the labor movement, as the proportion of union members has become increasingly composed of "white-collar" professionals (Asher et al. 2001, 28–29). Some recent organizing successes include workers who have virtually no history in the labor movement. In 1999, for example, some 15,000 doctors formed a union—the National Doctors Alliance. The powerful and influential American Medical Association also announced the formation of its own union (Kosterlitz 1999, 2477).

These changes have shifted power away from unions in the manufacturing sector, such as the United Steelworkers of America, which once held a key voice in the labor movement. According to the USWA, eighteen steel companies have filed for bankruptcy from 1997 to 2003, and nearly 18,000 steelworkers lost their jobs from January 1998 to July 2003. Indeed, unions now draw their strength from a different set of workers than they did when membership was at its height in the mid-1950s. The stereotype of the American "working-class hero," which once evoked images of the blue-collar factory worker, no longer reflects the typical union worker. Of course, manufacturing workers still maintain a healthy presence in the labor movement; however, the shift in power suggests that the future of organized labor now rests largely on the shoulders of workers in the public sector and to a lesser extent with workers in the service sector.

The occupational shifts in the labor movement, however, are not the only major changes that have affected the face and composition of the union workforce over the past half century. One major change has been in the diversity of the union workforce. An increasing number of women and minorities have now joined the union ranks.

Women in the Union Workforce

At the beginning of the twenty-first century, women made up a larger segment of the union workforce than they did at the beginning of the two previous decades. Women now represent roughly two of every five union workers, compared to one of every three union workers in the early 1980s. Indeed, women have been particularly receptive to organizing campaigns. In one survey, 49 percent of working women report that they would be willing to join a union, compared to 41 percent of working men (Nussbaum 1998, 59).

The rise of women in the union workforce has important implications for the labor movement in several respects. Perhaps most important, women have different perspectives from men on the largest problems facing the nation. A survey conducted by Peter D. Hart Research Associates (1998) asked respondents to rate the top problems in the nation on a ten-point scale, ten representing "extremely serious" problems. The results indicated that some 72 percent of women reported affordable health care coverage as a top concern (measured as at least an eight on their scale), as compared to 60 percent of men. Women also were more likely to express anxiety about savings and retirement. Sixty-four percent of women reported that a top problem facing the nation was the inability of people to save enough money for a secure retirement. By comparison, 43 percent of men viewed this as a top problem. Significant gender differences are also present on issues pertinent to the workforce. Roughly 61 percent of women viewed rising CEO salaries at the expense of jobs for regular employees as a top problem, compared to 43 percent of men. Likewise, 64 percent of women compared to 52 percent of men viewed an economy that allows the wealthy to do extremely well while average working people "just get by" as a top problem.

The fact that women have different perspectives about the seriousness of various problems facing the country may help explain why there are significant gender differences on policy initiatives concerning retirement security and health care. A slightly higher percentage of women than men support the idea of protecting the financial health of Social Security and protecting government health insurance for children whose parents cannot afford coverage (Hart 1998, 84). Given the significant gender differences in opinions on the major problems facing the nation and on various policy initiatives, it seems reasonable to conclude that not only has the face of the union worker changed, but also its voice. The fact that women are more troubled by economic inequality and are more willing to embrace government-style initiatives suggests that the future political agenda of the labor movement may well move in a more progressive direction.

Racial and Ethnic Diversity in the Union Workforce

Racial and ethnic minorities, specifically African Americans and Latinos, are a growing segment of the union workforce. Of the sixteen million union workers in the United States, roughly 2.3 million are African American. Unions have been particularly effective at unionizing African American workers. In 2004, the Bureau of Labor Statistics reported that 15.1 percent of African American workers belong to unions, compared to 12.2 percent of white workers (Bureau of Labor Statistics 2005). As African Americans become a larger percentage of the population over the next several decades, their numbers in the union workforce are likely to increase.

Latinos are also becoming a greater presence in the union workforce. Union membership among Latino workers has increased 20 percent during the last two decades (Wells 2000). Moreover, Latino immigrants have been increasingly receptive to organizing campaigns. As Andrew Gross Gaitan, a senior organizer of the SEIU, explains: "The immigrant workers are leading the way. They are the most militant, and that gives energy to the rest of the labor movement" (Mecoy 2000).

The rise of Latino immigrants in the labor movement, particularly in California, has had important political consequences. The state that once elected Richard Nixon to the U.S. Senate and Ronald Reagan as its governor has now become a beacon for progressive politics. According to Harold Meyerson (2004), a major reason for the transformation of California politics has been "the city's Latino-led labor movement, which mobilizes more Latino voters, anoints more Latino candidates, and constructs more progressive coalitions than any force in the state." Miguel Contreras, who heads the County Federation of Labor, is credited for registering hundreds of thousands new immigrant voters in California. Los Angeles County alone has sent five Latinos to the U.S. Congress, out of thirteen available seats. The labor-Latino coalition has been a boon to the Democratic Party in California, which controls both houses of the state legislature (Meyerson 2004). By comparison, Meyerson (2004) notes that cities such as Houston, Texas, have experienced similar increases in its Latino population but the city and state remain solidly Republican. In the absence of a strong labor movement to mobilize new immigrants, Latinos in Texas are largely removed from politics. Indeed, Houston is the largest Latino community in the nation without even a single representative in Congress.

Los Angeles and Houston thus provide instructive lessons for the future of American labor and politics. With racial and ethnic diversity likely to increase nationwide over the next several decades, there is certainly potential for a major national shift in a progressive direction. However, as the example of Houston illustrates, changing demographics alone will not bring about this shift toward more progressive politics. Any major change in American politics will rest heavily on mobilizing minorities, particularly new Latino immigrants. If unions can play a significant role in organizing minorities and new immigrants, as they have done in Los Angeles, then perhaps the prospects for a progressive shift in national politics are brighter than many political observers might realize.

Mobilizing the Rank and File in the Political Arena

Mobilization efforts, as the Los Angeles and Houston examples demonstrate, are important because union workers are not predisposed to engage in politics absent the encouragement and efforts of their union (Seidman, London, Karsh, and Tagliacozzo 1958). Union education and mobilization activities have a significant effect on the political participation of union members, even when controlling for factors such as socioeconomic status (Bok and Dunlop 1970). In fact, union grassroots efforts are sometimes so successful that voter turnout is frequently highest in U.S. states with the greatest share of workers represented by unions (Radcliff and Davis 2000).

While many local unions have led efforts to mobilize workers in cities such as Los Angeles, the national AFL-CIO has also made mobilization efforts a central component of its political efforts. In 1996, the AFL-CIO hired one hundred permanent union grassroots activists in each congressional district and recruited an additional 2,500 union activists and staff for the final six weeks of the election season for get-out-the-vote efforts. Sweeney also stepped up the AFL-CIO's grassroots efforts by establishing the National Labor Political Training Center. The center recruited more than 750 union volunteers for get-out-the-vote activities and political education efforts in competitive congressional districts (AFL-CIO 1999a). To mobilize union members to participate and vote for union-endorsed candidates, the AFL-CIO sent nine million pieces of direct mail in the general election and distributed flyers in 114 congressional districts. Local unions and central labor councils mailed an additional 2.5 million voter guides (Gerber 1999, 84).

Unions also worked in concert with Democratic Party committees, exchanging strategic campaign information and sponsoring voter contact drives (Rozell and Wilcox 1999, 25). The AFL-CIO further took advantage of the "Motor Voter" law, which provides voter registration forms at motor vehicle agencies, and contributed funds to nonpartisan voter registration projects (Gerber 1999, 85). It also worked in alliance with organizations such as Jesse Jackson's Rainbow Coalition to register minorities to vote (Lambro 1998). In 1998, grassroots expenditures were as high as $18 million, and included 300 full-time, paid activists (Bernstein and Dunham 1998, 53). In the final week of the 1998 election alone, the AFL-CIO sent seven million pieces of mail to union members urging them to vote. Union workers and volunteers made 14.5 million phone-calls for the AFL-CIO and local unions (Lawrence and Drinkard 1998).

Union affiliates were especially mobilized in 1998 because of several high-profile state and local issues, such as California's Proposition 226, which threatened organized labor. Proposition 226, also known as "paycheck protection," was a ballot initiative that would have required unions to receive preapproval from their members to have their dues used for political purposes. Local unions recruited 24,000 volunteers who made roughly 650,000 phone-calls to California voters explaining the effects of Proposition 226 and its potential to limit the political influence of unions (Berke 1998; AFL-CIO 1999a). Unions provided videotapes, held meetings at job sites, and made thousands of phone calls. The United Food and Commercial Workers (UFCW), for example, sent an anti-Proposition 226 video to 75,000 of its members (Bernstein, Borrus, and Brull 1998, 55). One video titled, "Corporate Takeover: The Truth About Proposition 226," opens with a grim warning for union members: "June 2 won't be a walk in the sun. . . . Big business and out-of-state corporations are ready to take over in California . . . if Proposition 226 passes in California." The presentation of the union's position in the video was also important. There was a concerted effort to explain the effects of the law from the perspective of the rank-and-file worker. One union official explained that member-to-member interactions were critical to the video's presentation: "Every single person in the video was a rank-and-file member. This was different from the past. Rank-and-file workers started talking to one another about the issues, and nothing works better than that" (Pérez 2000).

The video further encouraged union workers to spread the anti-Proposition 226 message to all California residents. As one UFCW clerk explained in the video, "Its important to me to let everybody know about 226, not just the people in the union, but my friends, my family, my neighbors—everybody has to know about this." Union members wore "anti-Prop 226" buttons and distributed pamphlets to fellow workers. These efforts were especially successful in persuading Republican union workers to vote against Proposition 226. Dan Terry, president of the California Professional Firefighters, remarked, "My union is 50 percent Republican, and they got it as clearly as anyone else. I believe we were probably at 80 percent or 85 percent in opposition by Election Day" (Bailey 1998). The final result was a clear rejection of Proposition 226 by California voters and a convincing and significant victory for unions. The Proposition 226 victory emboldened many unions and served as an important precursor to labor's 1998 campaign strategy. Sweeney remarked, "We gained a new strength and momentum heading into the fall elections" (Bernstein, Borrus, and Brull 1998, 55).

In 2000, the AFL-CIO spent upward of $40 million in seventy-one competitive congressional districts. It had 1,600 workers coordinating voter education programs in thirty-five states (Swoboda 2000). Unions registered 2.3 million new union household voters, made eight million phone calls to union households, and handed out more than fourteen million flyers and leaflets at union work sites. The national AFL-CIO alone sent more than twelve million pieces of direct mail to union households (AFL-CIO 2000b). The AFL-CIO continued to stress member-to-member contact. "We want to break it down to one-to-one, because talking about issues and candidates really works better on the shop floor when people hear it from someone they know," explained Duane McConville, who serves as the Steelworkers Local 19806 president (AFL-CIO 2000b). Organized labor's efforts even extended beyond union members. The AFL-CIO and AFSCME spent a combined $6 million on grassroots activities to mobilize African American and Latino voters. In some instances, labor sent trucks into minority neighborhoods trumpeting political messages (Hoffman 2000).

During the 2000 election, however, organized labor's political opponents began a grassroots offensive of their own. The Chamber of Commerce, one of the largest and most influential business organizations, sent a half million political mailings to its members (Lawrence and Drinkard 1998). Heading into the 2000 election, the Chamber's political director, David DiStefano, explained, "We will go on offense. We can reach three million businesses, and we intend to communicate our pro-business message for the 2000 elections" (DiStefano 1999).

Likewise, a coalition of business organizations reported that it would spend upwards of $7 million on advertising in 2000 in sixty-six competitive House districts to support vulnerable Republicans (Folkenflik 2000). Dennis Whitfield, the senior vice president of the National Federation of Independent Business (NFIB), explained: "It's pretty much black and white. . . . We've got a situation right now where the [GOP House] leadership has a 93 percent NFIB rating, and the speaker [J. Dennis Hastert] is 100 percent" (Edsall 2000). The Business Industry PAC (BIPAC) also unveiled Project 2000, which provided political education materials and "tool kits" to its members. The kits included software and voter guides that listed candidates' positions on twenty-five important business issues (Folkenflik 2000).

Conservative political organizations such as the National Rifle Association also countered labor's campaign activities by spending $25 million alone on its "Vote Freedom First" advertising campaign in the 2000 election. The NRA blanketed television with the message: "Vote freedom first! Don't risk having President Gore take away your gun" (Grady 2000). The NRA even attempted to weaken labor's 2000 campaign efforts by specifically targeting union members who own guns. NRA President Charlton Heston made several public appearances in which he urged union members to "remember only freedom, not what some shop steward . . . tells you." In Michigan, NRA activists posted fliers at auto factories that read, "Al Gore wants to ban guns in America." The AFL-CIO was forced to counter with flyers of its own that read, "Al Gore doesn't want to take away your gun, but George W. Bush wants to take away your union" (Brownstein 2000).

Despite the efforts of its political adversaries, organized labor was still able to generate a large turnout among its members. However, even with these impressive results, unions were unable to elect a Democratic majority to the House or Senate, and failed to stop Republican George W. Bush from winning the White House.

During the 2002 election, organized labor's campaign efforts again centered on grassroots activities. The AFL-CIO had 750 paid union officials and more than 4,000 local union coordinators working around the country on targeted campaigns. These coordinators and volunteers distributed more than seventeen million worksite fliers, sent fifteen million pieces of mail to union households, and made more than five million telephone calls. The AFL-CIO and its affiliates were active in forty-seven congressional races and sixteen Senate contests (AFL-CIO 2002).

The extensive grassroots efforts in the Sweeney era raise an important question: What effect did these grassroots activities have on the political participation and attitudes of union members? The answer, interestingly, appears to be mixed. Union members became more active in the political process; however, their political attitudes remained largely unchanged from the pre-Sweeney era.

Attitudes Toward Labor Unions and Big Business

Union educational campaigns are not only targeted to union members but also to their families. Unions send information to their members' households, and social gatherings that unions organize often involve the members' families. Thus, the effect of union efforts often extends beyond the members themselves. For this reason, it is important to look at the attitudes of all those who belong to union households.[3]

So how exactly did those in union households feel about labor unions and big business? Have the attitudes of those in union households changed since Sweeney's election? Using "feeling thermometer" questions from the American National Election Study (which asks individuals to rate political figures and groups from 0 to 100, with 100 as most favorable and 0 as least favorable), the results indicate that from 1988 through 2002, individuals who belonged to union households held more favorable opinions of labor unions than those in nonunion households. As figure 3.2 indicates, those from union households, on average, rated unions between 60 and 70 on a 100-point scale, while those in nonunion households scored unions in the low 50s.

The results, however, also reveal that there has been very little change in attitudes toward unions since Sweeney's election in 1995, including even those from union households. In fact, individuals from union households actually rated unions slightly lower in 2002 than in 1988 and the early 1990s, while the attitudes

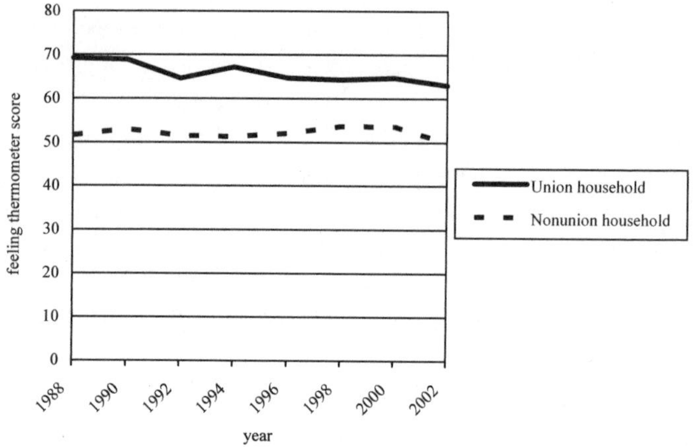

FIGURE 3.2 Average Feeling Thermometer Scores Toward Labor Unions

Source: American National Election Study.

Note: Feeling thermometer scores range from 0 to 100, with 100 representing favorable and 0 reflecting unfavorable.

of those from nonunion households remained about the same. These patterns were also similar when analyzing union members only (rather than the broader categorization of those from union households).

Several union scandals in the mid- to late 1990s were not helpful to labor's public image. Perhaps the most damaging scandal involved the Teamsters' leadership election in 1997. Former Teamsters president Ron Carey, who was elected president in 1991 as a self-proclaimed reformer, had his 1997 reelection victory overturned because of union election-law violations. Carey and his staff were accused of laundering Teamster funds for his reelection campaign against James P. Hoffa, the son of the famed former Teamsters' leader (Aronowitz 1998, 214). A court-appointed monitor forced a new election and banned Carey from running for reelection, resulting in a comfortable Hoffa victory a few months later. Months of bad publicity resulted from the controversy, likely reinforcing many of the negative public perceptions of labor unions and their leaders as corrupt and dishonest.

In 2002, the scandals at Enron, Global Crossing, and WorldCom seemed to present a historic opportunity for labor unions to make the case for the need of workers to organize into unions as a defense against corporate abuses. However, this effort was severely hampered when allegations surfaced that several union presidents were engaged in stock manipulation of their own at ULLICO, a union-supported insurance and investment company (Fritz 2002). As a result of the scandal, some union officials conceded that they no longer felt comfortable attacking corporate executives. Even Sweeney, they admitted, had "lowered his voice" on the issue (Fritz 2002). Of course, these scandals pale in comparison to those of past decades involving organized crime, and there have been several successes for unions during Sweeney's tenure. The aforementioned Proposition 226 was a major political and public relations victory for organized labor. In 1999, the largest union organizing victory in more than fifty years occurred when more than 74,000 home-care workers in Los Angeles voted 16,200 to 1,925 to unionize (St. Louis Post Dispatch 1999).

Still, the net results have been a wash. Since Sweeney's election, the public image of labor unions has not changed significantly, even among those in union households. Results from the Gallup News Service further confirm that overall public attitudes toward unions have changed little in recent years (see figure 3.3). In fact, the results reveal increased negative attitudes toward unions since the early 1960s. In 1961, for example, 69 percent of the public approved of labor unions, while just 20 percent disapproved. By the late 1970s, public approval began to fall and disapproval began to rise. In 1978, 59 percent of the public approved of labor unions compared to 31 percent who disapproved. The numbers have changed little since the late 1970s, with union approval at 58 percent and disapproval at 33 percent in 2002.

Attitudes toward big business have also remained relatively constant. Again using feeling thermometer questions from the American National Election Study, the results indicate that there has been little change in attitudes toward big business among indi-

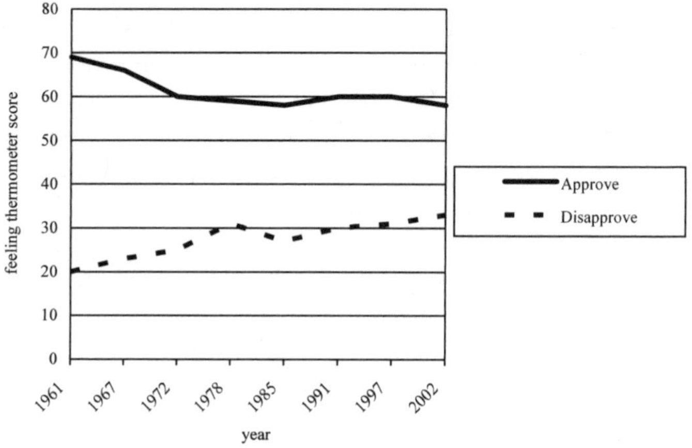

FIGURE 3.3 Public Approval of Labor Unions, 1961–2002

Source: Gallup Poll News Service.

Note: The "approve" and "disapprove" scores are based on respondents' answers to the following question: "Do you approve or disapprove of labor unions?"

viduals from union and nonunion households from 1988 to 2002 (see figure 3.4). Big business does not appear to have capitalized on the economic boom of the latter half of the 1990s; however, it suffered only a small drop following the numerous financial scandals at the beginning of the twenty-first century.

Taken together, the results suggest that organized labor has neither lost nor gained any ground in the battle of public relations with big business since Sweeney's election. Organized labor missed a historic opportunity to capitalize on the corporate scandals of 2002. Its own scandals of corruption, while much milder than in the past, continue to hinder its efforts to improve its image. The AFL-CIO is obviously limited in its ability to control corruption in local unions. However, the national leadership has taken some steps. When allegations surfaced that the union leadership of New York City's District Council 37 of AFSCME rigged a union vote on a city contract to win the favor of Republican mayor Rudolph Giuliani, Gerald

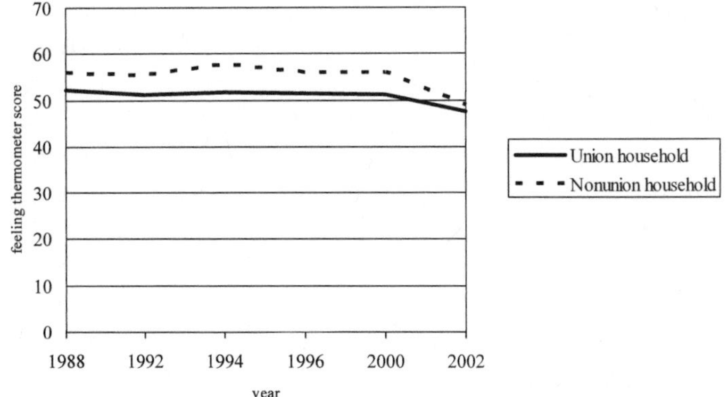

FIGURE 3.4 Average Feeling Thermometer Scores Toward Big Business

Source: American National Election Study.

Note: Feeling thermometer scores range from 0 to 100, with 100 representing favorable and 0 reflecting unfavorable.

McEntee, the national president of AFSCME, placed District Council 37 into receivership (Buhle 1999, 4–5). The national leadership of the AFL-CIO will need to continue to take a strong stand against union corruption, as the future of labor's public image will likely hinge on its ability to remain free of further scandals.

Political Attitudes and Voting Behavior

As reported in chapter 2, organized labor spends a disproportionate sum of its political funds to assist Democratic congressional candidates. Union campaign literature, flyers, direct mail, and advertising are typically more favorable to Democratic candidates than they are to Republican candidates. The AFL-CIO's extensive advertising and grassroots efforts under John Sweeney intensified those efforts. What effect did these efforts have on union members' attitudes toward the Democratic and Republican parties?

Using the previously mentioned feeling thermometer questions from the National Election Study, the results indicate that attitudes in union households toward the Democratic Party have not changed much over the past several years (see figure 3.5). Likewise, there have been only minor fluctuations in union household attitudes toward the Republican Party over the same period (see figure 3.6). These findings are understandable given that political attitudes, particularly those toward political parties, are typically stable in individuals throughout most of their lives (Converse 1966; Green and Palmquist 1994; but see Allsop and Weisberg 1988). Short-term forces, such as campaigns or political propaganda, rarely affect these attitudes. The AFL-CIO's efforts appear to be no exception.

Voting behavior and public support for candidates, on the other hand, is typically more fluid and subject to change as a result of campaign efforts (Bartels 1993; Finkel 1993). Sweeney made very little secret that one of the AFL-CIO's goals has been to help Democrats regain control of the U.S. Congress. Have union members been more likely to vote for Democratic candidates for Congress since Sweeney's election?

Data from the ANES reveal that union households have been solid supporters of Democratic House candidates throughout the period of 1988 to 2002 (see table 3.1). In most elections, more than 60 percent of those in union households supported Democrats for the House. This result is not surprising, given that decades of union political education efforts have produced a "union vote" that tips in favor of Democratic candidates (Campbell, Converse, Miller, and Stokes 1960; Axelrod 1972; Masters and Delaney 1987; Erikson, Lancaster, and Romero 1989).

What is perhaps more interesting is the widening gap between union and nonunion households. From 1988 to 1994, an average of 66.7 percent of union households reported voting for the Democratic candidate for the U.S. House compared to 55.1 percent in nonunion households, or a difference of 11.6 percent. From 1996 to 2002, 61.6 percent of union households reported voting for the Democratic candidate for the U.S. House compared to 46.4 percent in nonunion households, reflecting a somewhat larger difference of 15.2 percent.

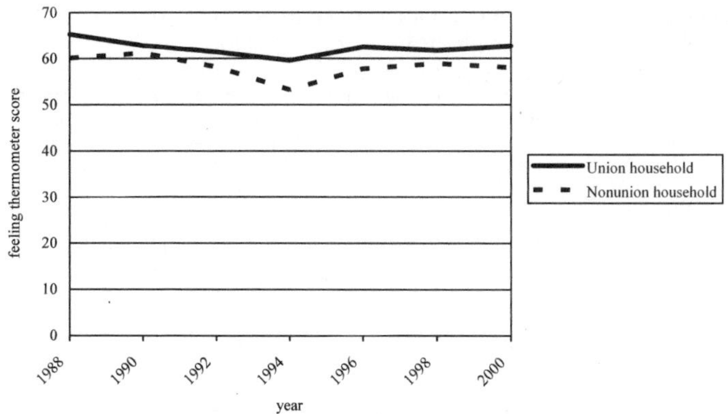

FIGURE 3.5 Average Feeling Thermometer Scores Toward the Democratic Party

Source: American National Election Study.

Note: Feeling thermometer scores range from 0 to 100, with 100 representing favorable and 0 reflecting unfavorable.

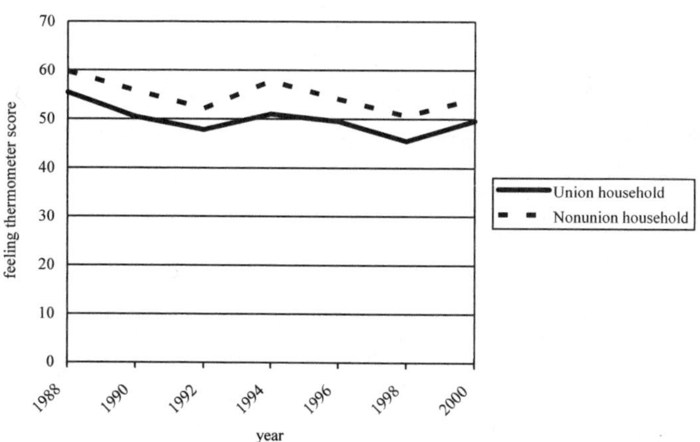

FIGURE 3.6 Average Feeling Thermometer Scores Toward the Republican Party

Source: American National Election Study.

Note: Feeling thermometer scores range from 0 to 100, with 100 representing favorable and 0 reflecting unfavorable.

TABLE 3.1 Percentage of Union and Nonunion Household Voters Who Voted Democratic or Republican for the U.S. House

YEAR	PARTY OF CANDIDATE	UNION HOUSEHOLD	NONUNION HOUSEHOLD	DEMOCRATIC ADVANTAGE
1988	Democrat	67.6%	56.9%	+10.7
	Republican	32.4	43.1	
1990	Democrat	72.4%	62.1%	+10.3
	Republican	27.6	37.9	
1992	Democrat	66.1%	57.9%	+8.2
	Republican	33.9	42.1	
1994	Democrat	60.8%	43.6%	+17.2
	Republican	39.2	56.4	
1996	Democrat	59.6%	46.1%	+13.5
	Republican	40.4	53.9	
1998	Democrat	57.1%	46.8%	+10.3
	Republican	42.9	53.2	
2000	Democrat	67.4%	48.8%	+18.6
	Republican	32.6	51.2	
2002	Democrat	62.1%	43.8%	+18.3
	Republican	37.9	56.2	

Source: American National Election Study.

These differences may even underestimate the actual gap between the two time periods. Estimates from Peter Hart Research Associates (1996, 1998, 2000, 2002), which draw from a much larger sample of union households than the ANES, indicate that union households voted for Democratic House candidates by much larger margins from 1996 to 2002. According to their data, 68 percent, 71 percent, 70 percent, and 68 percent of union households voted for Democratic House candidates in 1996, 1998, 2000, and 2002 respectively. Using these estimates, the gap separating union and nonunion households widens to 22.8 percent—a difference almost twice as large as that shown from 1988 to 1994.

Voting behavior in Senate elections fails to reveal any systematic changes from 1988 through 2002; however, the results do reinforce the overwhelming support that union households provide to

Democratic candidates (see table 3.2). Interestingly, Democratic support has remained strong among union members despite the fact that union members have become increasingly conservative in their political attitudes over time (Aronowitz 1983). The most plausible explanation for union members' steadfast support of Democratic candidates is that union political activities provide social cues and social pressure that can persuade them to vote in ways that they might otherwise decide differently if they were making the decision on their own (Asher et al. 2001, 146–151). Union political activities and mobilization efforts have helped to retain union members' support of Democratic candidates, even when ideological trends of union members or the voting behavior of nonunionized white males would suggest that union members should be voting Republican in greater numbers (Gottschalk 2000, 32). Indeed, union households have remained consistent supporters of Democratic candidates, even during elections in which the tide among nonunion households swung to Republicans. This raises the possibility that getting union members to the polls is likely to be a major factor in the success of Democratic candidates in congressional elections and raises the question: Has the AFL-CIO been able to improve its ability to mobilize and energize union members to participate in the political process?

Union Political Participation

One of the central elements of the AFL-CIO's new political program is its emphasis on member-to-member contact to mobilize its membership. The AFL-CIO's "People Powered Politics" program stresses the need of its membership to influence the participation and vote of other union members. As Steve Rosenthal, who became the political director of the AFL-CIO after Sweeney's victory, explains, "People talking to each other is the model. It is important to make politics more personal" (Rosenthal 2003). Has the AFL-CIO succeeded in getting its membership to become more involved in influencing the vote of family, friends, and coworkers?

TABLE 3.2 Percentage of Union and Nonunion Household Voters Who Voted Democratic or Republican for the U.S. Senate

YEAR	PARTY OF CANDIDATE	UNION HOUSEHOLD	NONUNION HOUSEHOLD	DEMOCRATIC ADVANTAGE
1988	Democrat	66.7%	54.5%	+12.2
	Republican	33.3	45.5	
1990	Democrat	79.7%	54.5%	+25.2
	Republican	20.3	45.5	
1992	Democrat	63.5%	53.6%	+9.9
	Republican	36.5	46.4	
1994	Democrat	58.7%	41.4%	+17.3
	Republican	41.3	58.6	
1996	Democrat	64.7%	49.6%	+15.1
	Republican	35.3	50.4	
1998	Democrat	68.3%	50.7%	+17.6
	Republican	31.7	49.3	
2000	Democrat	65.7%	53.5%	+12.2
	Republican	34.3	46.5	
2002	Democrat	61.4%	47.0%	+14.4
	Republican	38.6	53.0	

Source: American National Election Study.

The results in table 3.3 indicate that union households have become increasingly more likely than have those from nonunion households to influence the vote of others. The pre-Sweeney era (1988 through 1994) shows relative parity between union and nonunion households. In 1988, 31.3 percent of individuals from union households and 28.5 percent of those from nonunion households reported that they attempted to influence someone's vote—a difference of 2.8 percent. In 1990, nonunion households surpassed union households by 1.7 percent. Union households regained the advantage in 1992 and 1994 by 3.1 percent and 1.8 percent respectively. A year after Sweeney's election in 1996, however, the gap separating union and nonunion households rose to 6.6 percent. The margin increased to 6.8 percent in 1998, 9.9 percent in 2000, and 7.2 percent in 2002.

TABLE 3.3 Percentage of Union and Nonunion Household Voters Who Tried to Influence the Vote of Others

YEAR	UNION HOUSEHOLD	NONUNION HOUSEHOLD	DIFFERENCE
1988	31.3%	28.5%	+2.8
1990	15.9%	17.6%	-1.7
1992	39.9%	36.8%	+3.1
1994	23.4%	21.6%	+1.8
1996	32.9%	26.3%	+6.6
1998	24.9%	18.1%	+6.8
2000	42.6%	32.7%	+9.9
2002	33.9%	26.7%	+7.2

Source: American National Election Study.

These efforts appear to have helped unions get more of their members to the polls and increase their relative size in the electorate. During the last three presidential election years, union households have gradually increased as a percentage of the overall electorate. In 1992, union households composed 19 percent of the electorate, compared to 24 percent in 1996 and 26 percent in 2000 (Greenhouse 1996a; Greenhouse 2001). According to the AFL-CIO, there were 4.6 million more voters from union households in 2000 than in 1992. All the more impressive is that the number of voters from nonunion households fell by 15.5 million during the same period (Ayres 2001).

The numbers have also increased during the last three midterm elections. In 1998, voter turnout of union households accounted for 23 percent of the electorate, which marked a significant increase from the previous midterm election in 1994, when only 14 percent of the electorate came from union households (Galvin 1998; AFL-CIO 1999a). AFL-CIO estimates further indicate that there were 6.5 million more voters from union households in 1998 than in 1994 (Lambro 1998). Estimates for the 2002 election were not available because the Voter News Service experienced difficulties and was unable to provide exit polling. One estimate, however, reports union households again topped the 20 percent mark in 2002, accounting for roughly 21 percent of the electorate (Greenberg 2002). These patterns provide evidence of the success of organized labor's mobilization efforts. In the words of one political observer: "The union mobilization has stayed pretty consistent [since Sweeney's election] because the AFL-CIO and the big unions that always play in politics really do have it down to a science. They work very, very hard. . . . So you don't see much drop off on the union side in terms of intensity" (Magleby and Monson 2003, 25).

Summary

This chapter has examined changes that have occurred in the union workforce. The face of the union worker is quite different today from the stereotypical blue-collar worker of the 1950s. Union workers in the early twenty-first century are now likely to be employed in the government or public sector, rather than in the shop factory or on the assembly line. The union workforce is becoming more diverse, with two of every five union members being women, and with African Americans and Latino immigrants making up an increasing share of the union workforce. These changes are likely to have important political ramifications for the labor movement.

The rise of union members in the public sector leads to the obvious conclusion that the labor movement is likely to be increasingly supportive and protective of government jobs, agencies, and programs. The increasing number of women in the labor movement and their stronger support for government solutions to social problems such as health care suggests the possibility for an even stronger push by labor unions for expanded government social programs and services. A labor-led movement of racial and ethnic minorities also presents a potentially promising future for progressive Democratic candidates, as the political transformation of Los Angeles demonstrates.

In addition to the changes in the union workforce, the revamped political program of the AFL-CIO has succeeded in reenergizing union workers to participate in the political process. While political participation has dropped among nonunion households, those in union households have remained relatively active. Union households have made up a larger segment of the electorate since Sweeney's election, and have maintained their steadfast support for Democratic candidates despite rising support for Republican candidates in nonunion households.

The AFL-CIO has also increased its political expenditures in congressional elections. Organized labor continues to spend increasing sums of money on its political operations and is getting more from its membership than it was able to during the latter years of the Kirkland administration. However, Sweeney has been unable to stem declines in union density. Labor will need to improve on these efforts to strengthen their political influence. For labor to achieve its more far-reaching goal of electing a prolabor Congress, an expanded membership is essential. A larger and more mobilized labor movement might begin to shift the political balance away from its current conservative slant.

They've [business] got the money, but we've got something money can't buy. We've got the people.[1]

—JOHN SWEENEY

4

Countering Business

Union Campaigning in Congressional Elections

SAMUEL GOMPERS FIRST advanced the maxim that unions protect their friends and punish their enemies. In a letter to trade unionists, Gompers wrote, "We [labor] will stand by our friends and administer a stinging rebuke to men or parties who are either indifferent, negligent, or hostile, and, wherever opportunity affords, to secure the election of intelligent, honest, earnest trade unionists, with clear, unblemished, paid-up union cards in their possession" (Gompers [1906] 1978, 94–95). Unions have long worked to elect prolabor candidates by providing them with political resources, including campaign contributions, expenditures, and volunteers.

As the mid-1990s approached, critics began to charge that organized labor had become too reliant on its campaign contributions as its primary political resource. Steven Rosenthal explained what had become a common practice: "First, the local union invites the Democrat to a meeting with a dozen or so of its members. Then, the union's officer gives 'their man' the check. They shake hands and the candidate pats the officer on the back. Someone snaps a picture for the local newsletter. Drill over" (Rosenthal 1998, 99). This "drill" was problematic because by relying so heavily on campaign contributions, labor unions were playing to the strengths of their political opponents, notably the PACs and organizations in the business community, which easily outspend unions in most elections. In 2002, for example, corporate PACs contributed $29.3 million to Senate members and candidates and $70.3 million to House members and candidates. Labor PACs, by comparison, contributed significantly less, giving $8.6 million to Senate members and candidates and $45.3 million to House members and candidates (FEC 2003).

By attempting to compete in the "money game" of congressional elections, unions placed themselves at a distinct disadvantage. However, as noted in preceding chapters, the Sweeney leadership has made a concerted effort to invest more heavily in its human resources. Unions may not have the money to compete with business, but they have the manpower to help mitigate that disadvantage. This chapter considers the importance of union manpower in congressional elections. Specifically, what effect does union density have in congressional elections? In addition, unions have made changes in their political strategies during the Sweeney era, notably by spending more money on increased grassroots communications and independent expenditures. This chapter examines whether those changes have helped unions better compete against business and strengthen their influence in congressional elections.

The Financial Advantage of Business over Labor

Before the recent passage of the Bipartisan Campaign Reform Act (which became law immediately after the 2002 election), campaign contributions to federal candidates were regulated by the rules outlined in the original Federal Election Campaign Act. FECA allowed unions, corporations, trade associations, and other interest groups to establish PACs that can raise voluntary donations from their members or employees. The law defines a PAC as a committee or an association that receives contributions from more than fifty people and provides campaign contributions aggregating in excess of $1,000 during a calendar year or expenditures aggregating in excess of $1,000 during a calendar year to at least five federal candidates. A PAC may contribute no more than $5,000 to a federal candidate in a general or primary election. PACs have grown to become the second-largest source of campaign funds, trailing only individuals (Herrnson 2004).

Labor PACs have existed since the early twentieth century, when John L. Lewis, who served as president of the CIO, created Labor's Nonpartisan League (LNL). After Lewis left the CIO, its new president, Phillip Murray, replaced the LNL with the CIO-PAC. During the same period, labor's other major organization, the AFL, formed the Labor League for Political Education (LLPE). When the AFL and CIO merged in 1955, the LLPE and CIO-PAC became COPE, which continues to function as the primary electoral arm of the AFL-CIO (Wilcox 1994, 20; for more information about COPE, see chapter 1).

The national federations of various unions also have their own PACs. The PAC of the American Federation of State, County, and Municipal Employees, for example, is often the largest union contributor in congressional elections. According to the Federal Election Commission, AFSCME's PAC spent almost $8.5 million during the 2002 election cycle. Indeed, the total amount of money from all union PACs is substantial in congressional elections. Since the advent of FECA, labor PAC contributions have increased over time, reaching a combined high of $53.9 million to all U.S. House and U.S. Senate candidates.[2] Despite the tens of millions of dollars that union PACs contribute to congressional candidates, organized labor's investment pales in comparison to the amounts that corporate PACs contribute. As noted earlier, corporate PACs easily outspent labor PACs in the 2002 elections, and have dominated the money game since the 1980 election, outspending labor PACs by significant margins in U.S. House and Senate contests (see figure 4.1).

In addition to campaign contributions, political organizations, including those associated with organized labor, contribute what are referred to as "soft money" contributions. This money includes contributions that fall outside of the scope of federal law. Soft money is designed to promote "party-building" activities,

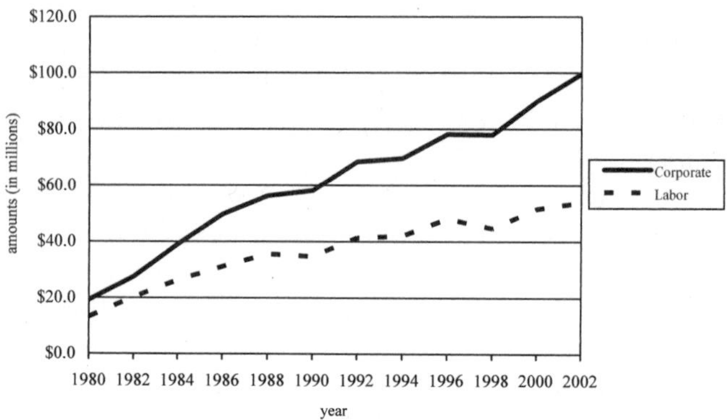

FIGURE 4.1 Labor and Corporate PAC Contributions to House and Senate Candidates

Source: Various FEC press releases.

Note: Amounts are based on the combined PAC contributions given to all candidates running for the U.S. House or the U.S. Senate, including retiring members. Dollar amounts are expressed in the millions.

such as get-out-the-vote drives and even television ads that support party platforms. Beginning in the mid-1990s, parties raised hundreds of millions of dollars through soft money channels.

Organized labor also took advantage of the soft money loophole. According to estimates from the Center for Responsive Politics, labor spent $35.9 million in soft money expenditures during the 2002 election. However, labor's rivals in the business sector outspent them by a rather wide margin. Interests affiliated with finance, insurance, and real estate spent roughly $92 million in soft money, while interests connected to other business interests spent an additional $51.8 million in soft money in 2002.

These hard and soft money totals exemplify the enormous financial disparities that separate organized labor and business. Unions simply cannot match the financial power of business groups. It is thus little wonder that labor's political influence began to wane in the 1980s and 1990s, when its political program during that time boiled down (in Rosenthal's own words) to giving "their man the check."

However, as Sweeney noted at the opening of the chapter, unions have the "people." Unions have made a considerable effort to mobilize their existing membership through grassroots activities, and unions have had success in increasing union household participation at the polls (see chapter 3). Nevertheless, the declines in union density represent an alarming development for organized labor, especially given the reality that it cannot compete dollar for dollar with business. To understand the importance of union density, the next section examines the relationship between union density and the success of labor's political allies—the Democrats—in congressional elections.

Union Manpower and the Democrats

Using the data from 1992 to 2000 (a period when union density data at the congressional district level were available; see Box-Steffensmeier, Arnold, and Zorn 1997), a simple, yet illustrative analysis reveals that Democrats have had remarkable success in unionized House districts. As the results in table 4.1 indicate, House districts with high levels of union density (districts with union density at 20.8 percent or higher) elected a Democrat to Congress 59 percent of the time. By comparison, House districts with medium levels of union density (districts with union density between 12.2 and 20.7 percent) and low levels of union density (districts with union density between 2.6 and 12.1 percent) elected a Democrat to Congress 52 percent and 46 percent of the time respectively.

These patterns were similar in Senate elections. In highly unionized states (defined as 17.5 percent or above), Democrats were successful 57 percent of the time. The Democrats' success rate fell to 53 percent in states with a medium level of union density (defined as 9.6 to 17.4 percent) and to 37 percent in states with a low level of union density (defined as 9.5 percent or less). Taken together, these numbers make clear that labor stands a markedly better chance of electing Democrats to the U.S. House and Senate when

TABLE 4.1 Union Density and Representation in Congress

	DISTRICT WITH LOW UNION DENSITY	DISTRICT WITH MEDIUM UNION DENSITY	DISTRICT WITH HIGH UNION DENSITY
HOUSE			
Democratic incumbent	45.9 %	51.8 %	59.0 %
Republican incumbent	54.1	48.2	41.0
SENATE			
Democratic incumbent	36.8 %	53.3 %	56.9 %
Republican incumbent	63.2	46.7	43.1

Chi-Square for House = 21.467***
Chi-Square for Senate = 6.446*

Note: The low, medium, and high categories for union density are divided into thirds. For the House, low union density falls between 2.6 percent and 12.1 percent; medium union density falls between 12.2 percent and 20.7 percent; and high union density falls at 20.8 percent and above. For the Senate, low union density falls between 3.5 percent and 9.5 percent; medium union density falls between 9.6 percent and 17.4 percent; and high union density falls at 17.5 percent and above. For the House, cases include Democratic candidates who ran for office during the 1992–2000 general election. These years were selected because union density data at the congressional district level were available for only those election cycles (see Box-Steffensmeier, Arnold, and Zorn 1997). For the Senate, union density data at the state level are available for the entire period under analysis. Cases therefore include Democratic candidates who ran for office during the 1988–2002 general election.
* $p < .05$, ** $p < .01$, *** $p < .001$.

they have more union workers in a congressional district or state. Added union manpower gained through more aggressive organizing strategies might well offset the financial advantage of business, increasing the prospects of Democrats regaining their majorities in both chambers of Congress.

Nevertheless, organizing workers is a long-term strategy. While union growth can occur quickly (see the discussion of "spurt theory" in chapter 2), it seems overly optimistic to assume that union density will increase as it did in the 1930s and 1940s, particularly given the many legal and illegal obstacles that union organizers confront on a regular basis. As Elaine Bernard, director of the

Harvard University Trade Union Program, aptly put it, "You're turning an oil tanker around, and it takes a long time to turn it" (Greenhouse 2000a).

For the more immediate future, unions have invested increasing amounts of their resources into mobilizing the members they do have. Of course, quantifying labor's mobilization efforts is a difficult assignment. Federal law does not require political organizations to report generic get-out-the-vote activities and expenditures. However, internal communications, such as direct mail, flyers, and phone-bank expenditures, are reported to the FEC when the expenditures exceed $2,000 on behalf of a candidate. The FEC defines these expenditures as "communication costs" that groups make directly to their members or employees. These communications either support or oppose a clearly identified candidate. Because the expenditures are designed to educate and mobilize the group's membership to participate in the political process, these expenditures seem an appropriate measure for grassroots mobilization efforts.

Independent expenditures are another component of labor's political efforts. These expenditures are made in complete independence of the candidate's campaign. There is no cooperation or consultation with the candidate or his or her authorizing committees. Independent expenditures typically pay for direct mail or television, radio, and newspaper advertisements that urge voters to support or oppose a candidate. These expenditures capture an important component of labor's media efforts in congressional elections.[3]

As noted in chapter 2, unions have invested increasing sums of money on grassroots mobilization efforts and independent expenditures since 1996. But have these increased expenditures helped organized labor counteract the power of business in congressional elections?

Labor Versus Business in Congressional Elections

There are four major avenues by which labor and corporate PACs attempt to influence congressional elections: (1) direct campaign contributions, (2) communication or grassroots expenditures, (3) independent expenditures, and (4) any remaining miscellaneous expenditures (e.g., in-kind contributions). When PACs distribute these resources in large sums to challengers and open-seat candidates, this can often improve electoral performance. The analysis that follows examines the effects of the net efforts of labor and corporate PACs on the electoral performance of Democratic House challengers and open-seat candidates.

Labor's Net Impact for Democratic House Challengers and Open-Seat Candidates

The level of assistance that Democratic House challengers and open-seat candidates receive from union PACs, and the level of assistance their opponents receive from corporate PACs, is likely to influence how well they perform in the general election. Specifically, the candidates who receive significantly more in direct campaign contributions, communication expenditures, independent expenditures, and any miscellaneous expenditures from unions than their opponents receive from corporate PACs should be the most likely to increase their share of the vote.

Of course, unions will only rarely have an advantage over business in campaign contributions. However, unions should consistently have a grassroots advantage, and in some contests, an advantage in independent expenditures over business. These latter two activities are therefore likely to be the most significant avenues for unions to mitigate the influence of business. Because communication and independent expenditures were a larger part of labor's budget in the Sweeney era, it seems reasonable to expect that unions did a better job of competing against business than they did in the Kirkland era.

However, to isolate the effects of labor's campaign efforts, other possible factors need to be controlled for when predicting a challenger or open-seat candidate's electoral performance. One very important factor is the candidate's own ability to raise and spend money in comparison to their opponent. Candidates who spend more money than their opponents are likely to wage stronger campaigns than those who are outspent by their opponents. Previous political experience is another important influence on electoral performance. Candidates who have experience serving as an elected public official or have unelected political experience typically wage the strongest campaigns (Jacobson 2001; Herrnson 2004). There are also district-level factors that can affect how well a candidate performs. The partisanship of the district is of obvious importance. Democratic candidates running in districts where voters have supported the Democratic presidential nominee are likely to stand a better opportunity of winning a greater share of the vote than are Democratic candidates in heavily Republican districts.

Other controls are needed for those who are open-seat candidates and those running in elections with three or more candidates on the ballot. Open-seat races are typically more competitive than incumbent-challenger contests, and elections with three or more candidates divide the vote across more candidates, which can reduce the candidate's vote percentage. Finally, candidates have historically been at a disadvantage if their party controls the White House in a midterm election year. Each of these factors is operationalized and analyzed in a multivariate statistical model (see the appendix for a specific definition of each measure).

The candidates included in the analysis ran for election from 1988 to 2002. Because a time-series cross-sectional analysis is necessary, traditional methods such as OLS may produce error terms that are heteroskedastic, autocorrelated, and contemporaneously correlated (Stimson 1985). To correct for this problem, the estimates are computed using generalized least squares (GLS). (For a more detailed explanation of the methodology, see the appendix.)

After controlling for each of the various factors mentioned above, the results indicate that a "union advantage" increases the share of the vote earned by Democratic House challengers and open-seat candidates (see table 4.2). These candidates gained an estimated .103 percent of the vote for every $10,000 (in 2002 dollars) that unions contributed more than business.[4] Democratic candidates also gained an increased share of the vote when unions outspent business on communications and independent expenditures.

However, one problem for Democratic challengers is that the campaign contributions they receive from labor rarely matches the contributions that their Republican opponents receive from

TABLE 4.2 GLS Estimates of the Net Effects of Union and Corporate Campaign Activities on Vote Shares for House Democratic Challengers and Open-Seat Candidates, 1988–2002

	COEFFICIENT	STANDARD ERROR
Labor contributions – opponent's corporate contributions (per $10,000)	.103***	.019
Labor communications – opponent's corporate communications (per $10,000)	.679***	.205
Labor independent expenditures – opponent's corporate independent expenditures (per $10,000)	.185**	.079
Labor miscellaneous expenditures – opponent's corporate miscellaneous expenditures (per $10,000)	– .600	.803
Expenditure advantage over opponent (per $100,000)	.155***	.030
Candidate has previous political experience	1.833***	.359
Partisanship of the district (pro-Democratic)	.646***	.024
Open-seat contest	6.559***	.466
Three or more candidates in election	– 2.779***	.371
Democratic president in power	– .823*	.434
Midterm election	1.106**	.422
Democratic president in power × midterm election	– 3.988***	.608
Constant	9.936***	1.233
(N)	(1,548)	
Wald Chi-Square	2,106.66***	
R2	.61	

Note: The dependent variable is the percentage of the vote received by the Democratic House challenger or open-seat candidate. All expenditures are indexed for inflation to reflect 2002 dollars. Cases include Democratic House challengers who ran in the 1988–2002 general election.

* $p < .05$, ** $p < .01$, *** $p < .001$.

Sources: The Federal Election Commission and various editions of the *Almanac of American Politics*.

business. In fact, even among the few Democratic challengers who defeated Republican incumbents, labor contributions, on average, failed to match the contributions that their opponents received from business. As table 4.3 indicates, the advantage that corporate PACs had over labor PACs in contributions, on average, reduced these Democrats' share of the vote by 0.3 percent in the Kirkland era and 0.4 percent in the Sweeney era.

Unions, however, were able to make up some of that lost ground through their grassroots communication expenditures. Labor typically outspends corporate PACs in this area. Moreover, grassroots efforts by business are less organized and usually less effective. Darrell Shull, the executive director of the Business-Industry Political Action Committee (BIPAC), conceded in 1998

TABLE 4.3 The Effect of Union Campaign Activities in Contests with a Winning Democratic House Challenger, 1988–2002

	KIRKLAND ERA	SWEENEY ERA	NET GAIN SWEENEY ERA
Average union – corporate contributions	–0.3	–0.4	–0.1
Average union – corporate communications	+0.2	+1.2	+1.0
Average union – corporate independent expenditures	0.0	+0.5	+0.5
Net union – corporate activities	–0.1	+1.3	+1.4
Number of Democratic nonincumbents who won with labor making the deciding difference	2	9	+7
Percentage of Democratic nonincumbents who won with labor making the deciding difference	11 %	31 %	+20 %

Note: Top half numbers reflect the estimated gain or loss in Democratic House challengers' vote shares. The estimates are based on the coefficients in table 4.2, and reflect the differences between the average level of union assistance Democratic House challengers received and the average level of corporate assistance their opponent received.

that there were "incidents of business groups doing issue ads and some grassroots work, but there were no integrated strategies" (Kruger 2000, 35).

While unions often do a more effective job than business with grassroots work, labor failed to invest a significant amount of money in this area during the Kirkland era. Labor's grassroots efforts in the Kirkland era helped Democratic challengers gain an average of only 0.2 percent of the vote. By comparison, the larger investment in grassroots communication expenditures during the Sweeney era translated into a much larger average gain of 1.2 percent of the vote.

The same patterns were present with independent expenditures. Unions held no significant advantage over corporate PACs in independent expenditures during the Kirkland era and thus received no appreciable gain in the vote. The increased sums of money spent on independent expenditures during the Sweeney period, however, increased the share of the vote by 0.5 percent for Democratic candidates.

Taken together, these results confirm that unions simply cannot match business dollar for dollar in PAC contributions. However, they can compete in the electoral arena against business when they invest in efforts to mobilize their members through communication expenditures and to influence the campaign agenda through independent expenditures. Unions during the Kirkland era lost ground to business because their political efforts focused primarily on campaign contributions. On the other hand, during the Sweeney era, unions invested significantly more resources into communications expenditures, which played to labor's strength in manpower, and allowed unions to counter effectively the financial advantage of business.

This shift in resources had significant implications in the races in which Democratic challengers were ultimately successful. During the Kirkland period, eighteen Democratic House challengers won their election, but only two of those candidates—11 percent—appear to have won their election because of the assistance they received from organized labor. By comparison, twenty-nine Democratic House challengers won their election during the

Sweeney period, but nine of those candidates—31 percent—appear to have won their election because of the assistance they received from organized labor. These results reinforce the conclusion that organized labor's shift in resources during the Sweeney era helped a greater percentage of House Democratic challengers win their elections.

One instructive example of labor's effect in congressional elections was in the tenth district of Ohio during the 1996 election. The district, which included the areas of the west side of Cleveland and the western suburbs of Cuyohoga County, was represented by two-term Republican incumbent Martin Hoke (Barone and Ujifusa 1997, 1127). Hoke, who had won the previous election in 1994 by 13 percentage points, was opposed by Dennis Kucinich, who twenty years earlier had served as the mayor of Cleveland. Kucinich drew strong support from organized labor for his strong opposition to the free trade agreements NAFTA and GATT, and Kucinich in turn embraced his association with unions, noting he was "from the house of labor" and the "family of labor" (Barone and Ujifusa 1997, 1128).

The AFL-CIO ran several ads in the district critical of Hoke's record on labor issues. The congressman, in turn, responded by claiming that the ad campaign against him was built on "massive lying and disinformation" (Diemer 1996). Union independent expenditures on media and advertising had a limited effect after considering the counterefforts of business on behalf of Hoke. Interestingly, union contributions actually exceeded Hoke's corporate contributions; however, the largest effect on the election results came from labor's grassroots communications. Labor's grassroots communications accounted for 93 percent of all the communications assistance received by Kucinich and helped him win an estimated 3.2 percent more of the vote. Kucinich ultimately won the election by 3 percentage points, 49 to 46 percent. Without labor's strong grassroots mobilization effort on behalf of Kucinich, it is likely that Hoke would have won the election.

In open-seat contests with a successful Democratic candidate, union contributions sometimes exceeded business contributions; however, unions gained a more significant advantage over business in the Sweeney era, with its increased investment on communication expenditures (see table 4.4). This resulted in a slightly higher percentage of successful Democratic open-seat candidates winning their election because of the efforts of labor. During the Kirkland era, from 1988 to 1994, roughly 7 percent of the successful Democratic open-seat candidates won because labor's efforts created a net advantage over business. From 1996 to 2002, however, labor's increased grassroots efforts helped it outduel business in a larger percentage of contests. In the Sweeney era, 12 percent of the successful Democratic open-seat candidates won due to labor's efforts. This may seem like only a modest effect, but with Congress so closely divided between Republicans and Democrats, every seat counts. More important, the results indicate a positive trend in the Sweeney era. Despite declines in union membership, labor has been remarkably successful in maintaining an important role in congressional elections.

An open-seat contest in the 1998 elections in Colorado's second congressional district provides a helpful illustration of labor's effect. Democrat Mark Udall, a Colorado state House member and the son of former Arizona Congressman Morris Udall, and Republican Robert Greenlee, the mayor of Boulder and owner of the Rock Bottom Brewery and Black Hawk casino, emerged as the two major-party candidates vying to fill the seat vacated by incumbent Democrat David Skaggs. Greenlee invested $1 million of his personal wealth in the campaign, and had a total campaign warchest of $1.9 million. During the election, Greenlee labeled global warming theories "phony science" and campaigned on probusiness themes (Barone and Ujifusa 1999, 329).

Udall, in contrast, supported striking telephone workers at U.S. West Communications in August of the election season. At a rally, Udall commented, "It seems crazy to me that U.S. West would be so short-sighted to put you [the workers] in this position. It seems to me that that it makes good business sense to take care of employees." Union leader Rene Tafolla vowed that union workers would "remember" Udall's appearance and support for the workers "come election time" (George 1998). Udall received more PAC money from organized labor than other sector in the interest group community.[5] Unions contributed slightly more money to

TABLE 4.4 The Effect of Union Campaign Activities in Contests with a Winning Democratic House Open-Seat Candidate, 1988–2002

	KIRKLAND ERA	SWEENEY ERA	NET GAIN SWEENEY ERA
Average union – opponent's corporate contributions	+0.8	+0.7	–0.1
Average union – opponent's corporate communications	+0.2	+0.7	+0.5
Average union – opponent's corporate independent expenditures	0.0	+0.2	+0.2
Net union – opponent's corporate activities	+1.0	+1.6	+0.6
Number of Democratic nonincumbents who won with labor making the deciding difference	7	8	+1
Percentage of Democratic nonincumbents who won with labor making the deciding difference	7 %	12 %	+5 %

Note: Top half numbers reflect the estimated gain or loss in Democratic House open-seat candidates' vote shares. The estimates are based on the coefficients in table 4.2, and reflect the differences between the average level of union assistance Democratic House open-seat candidates received and the average level of corporate assistance their opponent received.

Udall than corporations did for Greenlee; however, Udall's most significant advantage came from labor's advantage over business in its investment in communications and independent expenditures. Labor's greater allocation of resources into communications and independent expenditures helped Udall win an estimated 4 percent more of the vote, contributing to his narrow victory over Greenlee, 50 to 47 percent.

In 2002, Democrat Michael Michaud earned a close 52 to 48 percent victory over Republican Kevin Raye in Maine's second congressional district. Michaud, a state legislator, had spent twenty-eight years as a union member working at the paper mill, Great Northern Paper. Michaud actively campaigned on workers' issues and embraced support from unions, noting that he would rather accept money and assistance from "working-class people because their interests are the same as mine: wanting a good job, good benefits, good wages, and a chance to make a decent living" (Jansen 2002). Labor's overall expenditures in this contest far outstripped the counterefforts of business. Michaud earned roughly 6 percent more of the vote because of labor, with two-thirds of that amount coming from labor's grassroots communications. Labor's net advantage over business, particularly with respect to its grassroots campaign, accounted for Michaud's margin of victory.

These results make clear that when unions focus all of their efforts on campaign contributions, the financial advantage of business can overwhelm their support. However, unions have a much greater effect on congressional elections when they focus their efforts on grassroots communications and, to a lesser extent, independent expenditures. As the Sweeney era demonstrates, labor's increased expenditures on grassroots communications and independent expenditures helped tip an increasing percentage of elections in favor of Democrats—races that otherwise might have been Republican victories.

Assisting Democratic House Incumbents

Congressional House incumbents win reelection more than 90 percent of the time. Many do not even face an opponent in the general election. In 2002, for example, there were seventy-eight House incumbents who went unchallenged by a major-party challenger (Herrnson 2004, 30). Even when faced with a major-party challenger, incumbents often win by comfortable margins. The average margin of victory for a House incumbent was thirty-four points (66 percent to 32 percent) from 1988 to 2002.[6]

While most incumbents are likely to win easily, there are some who face very competitive challengers. These incumbents typically ask political organizations such as labor PACs and organizations to contribute money and assistance to their campaigns. Labor PACs, which want to "protect their friends," are often willing and eager to assist a congressional ally in need of their assistance (Saltzman 1987; Burns, Francia, and Herrnson 2000).

However, replicating the previous analysis for incumbents presents a major difficulty: unions provide the most assistance to the incumbents who are in the most jeopardy. As a result, there is an inverse relationship between union contributions and expenditures and the percentage of the vote received by the incumbent. Yet, as many Democrats could attest, it would certainly be a mistake to conclude that unions are not helpful to a vulnerable incumbent's campaign. Vulnerable Democratic incumbents certainly need all the resources they can possibly obtain, and labor's ability to target their resources to these candidates can be very important in tipping the balance of a close election.

Not surprisingly, unions, on average, contribute and spend more of their resources (i.e., contributions, communications expenditures, independent expenditures, and other miscellaneous expenses) in competitive contests than they do in uncompetitive contests. From 1988 to 2004, Democratic incumbents in contests decided by twenty points or less received an average of $158,000 in total union campaign assistance, compared to $91,000 for incumbents in safe races decided by more than twenty points.[7] In races decided by ten points or less, the most "vulnerable" incumbents received an average of $178,000 in total union assistance, compared to $99,000 for incumbents in races decided by more than ten points.

The above numbers certainly give credence to the notion that unions do in fact protect their friends. However, as noted in chapter 2, unions since Sweeney's election have expanded their political operations. Have vulnerable Democratic incumbents been better "protected" under the Sweeney leadership? Have they been able to counter the efforts of corporate PACs?

With Republicans in control of the House after the 1994 elections, many corporate PACs became increasingly willing to assist promising Republican challengers. The results in table 4.5 confirm this. Corporate PACs increased their average support to promising Republican challengers from $34,202 in the Kirkland era, which was before Republicans won control of the U.S. House, to $60,587 in the Sweeney era. Unions, however, responded by providing more campaign assistance to vulnerable Democratic incumbents in the Sweeney era than in the Kirkland era. Labor organizations contributed and spent 19 percent more on vulnerable Democratic incumbents, increasing their average support from $168,494 in the Kirkland era to $201,187 in the Sweeney era and offsetting the increases made by business. Had labor failed to respond to the increases made by corporate PACs, it seems reasonable to believe that Republicans would likely have expanded their majorities in the U.S. House from 1996 to 2002.[8]

Labor's Net Effect on Democratic Senate Challengers and Open-Seat Candidates

In addition to the significant investment that unions make in House elections, they also contribute and spend significant resources in U.S. Senate elections. Using the same methods and controls as presented in table 4.2, the net effect of union activities compared to business activities is examined in Senate elections involving Democratic challengers and open-seat candidates. According to the es-

TABLE 4.5 Labor and Corporate PAC Campaign Contributions and Expenditures in House Elections Involving Vulnerable Democratic Incumbents, 1988–2002

	KIRKLAND ERA (1988–1994)	SWEENEY ERA (1996–2002)	AMOUNT ($) INCREASE
Corporate PAC $ to opponent	$34,202	$60,587	$26,383
Union PAC $	$168,494	$201,187	$32,693

Note: Union contributions and expenditures include all direct contributions, in-kind contributions, coordinated expenditures, independent expenditures, communication expenditures, and other miscellaneous expenditures on behalf of the candidate. Independent and communication expenditures against a candidate's opponent are also treated as expenditures on behalf of the candidate. Amounts are indexed for inflation to reflect 2002 dollars. Cases include Democratic House incumbents who were in contests decided by 10 points or less in the 1988–2002 general election.

timates in table 4.6, Democratic challengers and open-seat candidates were able to increase their share of the vote when unions outspent corporate PACs on grassroots communications. The insignificant results for contributions and independent expenditures suggest that the large sums of money spent by union PACs on these activities was cancelled out by the large sums of money spent by corporate PACs on those same activities. Grassroots communications were the exception, because union PACs invested significantly more money in this effort than did corporate PACs. These results once again reinforce the crucial importance of grassroots activities for the labor movement in congressional elections.

Not surprisingly, labor's increased investment on grassroots efforts during the Sweeney era had important political results. Of the successful Senate Democratic nonincumbents, labor's increased grassroots efforts netted an average gain of 2.8 percent of the vote in the Sweeney era compared to a 1 percent gain in the Kirkland era (see table 4.7). In addition, a much higher percentage of those candidates owe their victories to labor during the Sweeney era than during the Kirkland period. Two of the thirteen Democratic Senate nonincumbents—15 percent—who won their elections during the Kirkland period would have failed without labor's efforts. By comparison, twelve of twenty-one Democratic Senate nonincumbents—57 percent—would have failed without labor's efforts during the Sweeney period.

The Michigan Senate contest in 2000 provides an illustration of how labor can have a significant effect on Senate elections. Republican Spencer Abraham won a seat to the U.S. Senate in 1994, but faced a competitive challenge from former House member Debbie Stabenow. Corporate contributions on behalf of Abraham swamped union contributions on behalf of Stabenow by more than $1 million. However, unions spent nearly $100,000 on grassroots communications, helping Stabenow overcome and surpass the huge financial efforts of business on Abraham's behalf. Labor's grassroots efforts were particularly effective because Election Day is a paid holiday for autoworkers in Detroit. This helped generate a very large union turnout. Roughly 43 percent of the Michigan electorate came from union households in the 2000

TABLE 4.6 GLS Estimates of the Net Effects of Union and Corporate Campaign Activities on Vote Shares for Senate Democratic Challengers and Open-Seat Candidates, 1988–2002

	COEFFICIENT	STANDARD ERROR
Labor contributions – opponent's corporate contributions (per $10,000)	.038	.024
Labor communications – opponent's corporate communications (per $10,000)	.491***	.155
Labor independent expenditures – opponent's corporate independent expenditures (per $10,000)	.067	.128
Labor miscellaneous expenditures – opponent's corporate miscellaneous expenditures (per $10,000)	–.139	.783
Expenditure advantage over opponent (per $100,000)	.018*	.011
Candidate has previous political experience	2.654*	1.367
Partisanship of the district (pro-Democratic)	.386***	.105
Open-seat contest	2.932*	1.454
Three or more candidates in election	–.703	1.446
Democratic president in power	–2.240	1.609
Midterm election	–3.794*	1.828
Democratic president in power × midterm election	–.260	2.434
Constant	24.651***	5.525
(N)	(160)	
Wald Chi-Square	86.45***	
R2	.40	

Note: The dependent variable is the percentage of the vote received by the Democratic House challenger or open-seat candidate. All expenditures are indexed for inflation to reflect 2002 dollars. Cases include Democratic House challengers who ran in the 1988–2002 general election.

$p < .05$, ** $p < .01$, *** $p < .001$.

Sources: The Federal Election Commission and various editions of the *Almanac of American Politics*.

TABLE 4.7 The Effect of Union Campaign Activities in Contests with a Winning Democratic Senate Challenger or Open-Seat Candidate, 1988–2002

	KIRKLAND ERA	SWEENEY ERA	NET GAIN SWEENEY ERA
Average union – opponent's corporate contributions	0.0	0.0	0.0
Average union – opponent's corporate communications	+1.0	+2.8	+1.8
Average union – opponent's corporate independent expenditures	0.0	0.0	0.0
Net union – opponent's corporate activities	+1.0	+2.8	+1.8
Number of Democratic nonincumbents who won with labor making the deciding difference	2	12	+10
Percentage of Democratic nonincumbents who won with labor making the deciding difference	15 %	57 %	+42 %
(N)	(13)	(21)	

Note: Top half numbers reflect the estimated gain or loss in Democratic Senate challengers' and open-seat candidates' vote shares. The estimates are based on the coefficients in table 4.4, and reflect the differences between the average level of union assistance Democratic Senate challengers and open-seat candidates received and the average level of corporate assistance their opponent received.

election (Labor Research Association 2000). Labor's impressive grassroots and get-out-the-vote efforts helped Stabenow win an estimated 1 percent more of the vote, which was the crucial difference in her victory over Abraham.

As the Stabenow election and the overall results suggest, unions can overcome the financial advantage of business in Senate elections when they invest their resources into mobilizing their members through grassroots communications. Moreover, labor's increased investment in grassroots communications during the Sweeney era has helped several Democratic challengers and open-seat candidates win office to the U.S. Senate. The Senate results confirm that without labor's more intensive grassroots efforts under Sweeney, it is likely that Senate Republicans would have enjoyed greater success following the elections from 1996 through 2002.

Assisting Democratic Senate Incumbents

Senate incumbents typically face stronger challengers than House incumbents, and as a result are more likely to be involved in competitive elections. Business organizations assisted promising Republican challengers, increasing their contributions and expenditures an average of 39 percent from $343,610 during the Kirkland era to $478,406 during the Sweeney era (see table 4.8). Unions, however, responded by contributing and spending an average of 23 percent more on vulnerable Democratic incumbents during the Sweeney era than they did during the Kirkland era. Union contributions did not keep pace with business contributions, but without labor's counterefforts, Democrats may have lost several close contests in the U.S. Senate, providing even larger Republican majorities.

The Future of Organized Labor Under BCRA

After the 2002 election, Congress reformed federal campaign finance laws, which included a ban on soft money donations to political parties. Section 101 of the Bipartisan Campaign Reform Act (BCRA) adds a new section (section 323) to federal law that, among several provisions, "forbids the national party committees from soliciting a contribution of 'soft money' by a donor to any other party, committee, or organization of any kind." Since Sweeney's election, the AFL-CIO had become a significant soft money contributor to Democratic Party committees. With the enactment of BCRA, organized labor was forced to redirect its money to other channels.

TABLE 4.8 Labor and Corporate PAC Campaign Contributions and Expenditures in Senate Elections Involving Vulnerable Democratic Incumbents, 1988–2002

	KIRKLAND ERA (1988–1994)	SWEENEY ERA (1996–2002)	AMOUNT ($) INCREASE
Corporate PAC $ to opponent	$343,610	$478,406	$134,796
Union PAC $	$365,086	$449,541	$84,455

Note: Union contributions and expenditures include all direct contributions, in-kind contributions, coordinated expenditures, independent expenditures, communication expenditures, and other miscellaneous expenditures on behalf of the candidate. Independent and communication expenditures against a candidate's opponent are also treated as expenditures on behalf of the candidate. Amounts are indexed for inflation to reflect 2002 dollars. Cases include Democratic Senate incumbents who were in contests decided by 10 points or less in the 1988–2002 general election.

A popular vehicle in the 2004 election cycle was to funnel money through so-called "527" organizations, which received their name because they fall under section 527 of the Internal Revenue Code. A 527 group is exempt from taxation, although contributions to these organizations are not tax deductible. It can accept unlimited donations from unions, corporations, or wealthy individuals—similar to the "soft money" donations that poured into the national party organizations' coffers before the passage of BCRA. A 527 organization can spend its donations on issue advocacy advertisements and get-out-the-vote efforts, just as national party organizations could do prior to BCRA.

For organized labor, 527 organizations replaced the Democratic Party's national, senatorial, and congressional committees as conduits for union get-out-the-vote expenditures. The Partnership for America's Families and Voices for Working Families are two major 527 organizations with connections to organized labor that have emerged from the BCRA reforms. The real significance of this development, however, is that unlike traditional union efforts that target union members for get-out-the-vote efforts, these groups used their funds to target progressive voters who are not union members, including African Americans, Latinos, and women.

Indeed, in February 2003, the Partnership for America's Families announced that it would spend $20 million to mobilize progressive voters in an effort to build a wider coalition against the policies of the Bush administration. As Sweeney explained, "[The Bush] administration has actively sought every opportunity to pull the rug out from under working Americans, including slashing health and safety, stripping bargaining rights from federal workers and now putting overtime pay and the Federal Medical Leave Act in its sights" (Edsall 2003). Originally, the AFL-CIO, the SEIU, and AFSCME formed the core of the Partnership for America's Families. However, in May 2003, an internal dispute between former AFL-CIO political director Steve Rosenthal and AFSCME President Gerald McEntee concerning outreach efforts to minority communities led to the creation of Voices for Working Families.

The Partnership for American Families underwent a major restructuring in September 2003, when it announced that would merge into a broader group consisting of environmental and women's groups. Funded by billionaire financier George Soros, the new organization, Americans Coming Together (ACT), pledged to spend $75 million on get-out-the-vote efforts in seventeen states for the 2004 election (Cillizza 2003). Steve Rosenthal served as the CEO of ACT. With its strong financial backing from Soros, ACT was one of the most formidable progressive organizations during the 2004 election.

Two other groups with labor ties, Grassroots Democrats and America Votes, also played an important role in the 2004 election. America Votes is a coalition of several prominent unions, such as AFSCME and the SEIU, and environmental groups, including the Sierra Club. Grassroots Democrats, headed by Amy Chapman, who served as a campaign director with the AFL-CIO, pledged to funnel its group's money to assist Democratic local and state party organizations with get-out-the-vote efforts. Grassroots Democrats worked in cooperation with the Association of Trial Lawyers of America (ATLA). The board of Grassroots Democrats included Linda Lipson, the senior director for public affairs of ATLA.

These various 527 organizations underscores how the labor movement has evolved. Instead of withdrawing from coalitions as it once did, particularly in the early 1970s, the labor movement has led the charge to bring the progressive community together. Organized labor began moving in this direction soon after Sweeney's election, and the recent reforms of the campaign finance system have brought this development into full swing. The coalition of organized labor, minority voters, trial lawyers, environmentalists, and women's groups—all working together in various combinations—brought together progressive forces for the 2004 election. The rise of various 527 organizations following BCRA, and labor's central role in all of them, demonstrates how organized labor has clearly become an important leader of the larger progressive movement.

Summary

Organized labor relies on a number of political resources to influence congressional elections. Unions contribute money to candidates, sponsor advertisements, and mobilize their members to participate in the political process. During the late 1980s and early 1990s, labor relied predominantly on its cash contributions to influence elections. The enormous wealth of the business sector, however, overwhelmed labor's financial resources and weakened its political influence in congressional elections.

Beginning in the mid-1990s, the AFL-CIO, under John Sweeney, restructured its political program by investing more money in grassroots mobilization and advertising. These efforts have had an important effect in both House and Senate elections. In particular, organized labor's expanded grassroots campaign has been especially helpful for Democratic challengers and open-seat candidates, who in several competitive races have been able to counter the money that business provides Republican candidates. This is not to suggest that unions are more powerful than business organizations. Rather, the underlying lesson of this chapter is that unions can better compete and occasionally succeed when they invest in efforts to mobilize and educate their membership. Business has the money, but as Sweeney reminds us, unions have the people. When labor focuses its resources on its manpower, unions are able to overcome the financial advantage of business, and can sometimes have a significant effect on the outcome of congressional elections.

Yet despite labor's increased grassroots efforts since Sweeney's election, Republicans have maintained their majority status in the House and Senate (with the exception of the 107th Congress in the Senate) since the 1994 election. This is not to suggest that the failures of the Democratic Party are the result of any failures on the part of labor. In fact, the results in this chapter suggest that Democrats would likely be even further entrenched as a minority party were it not for the campaign efforts and assistance of organized labor.

Nevertheless, the 2002 elections marked the first election in the Sweeney era in which Democrats failed to pick up seats in the House of Representatives. Ironically, labor's political opponents appear to have used labor's own grassroots strategy against them. In 2002, Republicans invested significant sums of money in get-out-the-vote efforts. The Republican National Committee and the Republican state party committees jointly funded the "72-Hour Taskforce," which invested in mobilization efforts of Republican voters in the final three days of the 2002 election (Magleby and Monson 2003). The efforts helped increase Republican turnout and played a role in mitigating the Democrats' efforts to mobilize their base of voters, contributing to the Republicans' success (Balz and Allen 2002).

Unions must continue to invest in grassroots mobilization efforts. However, to win back control of the Congress, unions must do even more. Republicans and their allies have effectively responded to labor's ground war by mobilizing their own supporters. Labor must expand its ranks if it is to win in the political arena.

We're happy that we won in a lot of Congressional races. . . . It [issue advertising] was money well-spent.[1]

—JOHN SWEENEY, PRESIDENT OF THE AFL-CIO

5

The Air War

The AFL-CIO Advertising Campaign

WHILE ORGANIZED LABOR has long spent money on contributions, communications, and independent expenditures to influence congressional elections, the AFL-CIO popularized the use of so-called "issue advocacy" advertisements shortly after Sweeney became president of the organization in 1996. The AFL-CIO ads drew fierce attacks from Republicans, who accused labor of trying to buy the 1996 election. A briefing paper from the House Republican Conference noted, "Not since the days of Jimmy Hoffa have they [unions] shown such naked ambition, brazen disregard for federal campaign law, and raw political power" (Toner 1996).

However, the effectiveness of the AFL-CIO advertising campaign in congressional elections is not entirely clear. On the one hand, critics of the advertising campaign argue that unions simply cannot afford to compete in the high-priced air wars of political campaigning. Rick Bender, president of the Washington State Labor Federation, explained, "Unless we [unions] are willing to saturate the airwaves, which we could never afford to do, we can't compete on that level." Gerry Shea, government affairs assistant to Sweeney, in reference to high-priced media campaigning, candidly added, "We know we can't win that game" (Sobieraj 1999).

On the other hand, there is some research to suggest otherwise. According to estimates from political scientist Gary Jacobson (1999), the AFL-CIO's 1996 issue ad campaign decreased the share of the vote for targeted freshmen Republicans by an average of 4.3 percentage points. Jacobson writes that "without labor's help, the 1996 elections would have been an even greater disappointment to the Democrats. If we subtract the additional vote for Democratic challengers opposing Republican freshmen attributed by the equation . . . to the AFL-CIO's campaign, only five of the 12 victors would have won" (Jacobson 1999, 193).

This chapter therefore examines whether the AFL-CIO issue advertising campaign had a significant effect in congressional elections. Because these ads were not a major part of the AFL-CIO's political efforts during Kirkland's tenure, this chapter focuses solely on the Sweeney period. It covers the effects of the AFL-CIO advertising campaign in the 1996, 1998, 2000, and 2002 congressional elections.

An Overview of the AFL-CIO's Advertising Campaign (1996–1998)

In 1996, the AFL-CIO established a new media fund that allocated $35 million for paid media on "issue advocacy" advertisements (Beck, Taylor, Stranger, and Rivlin 1997). This advertising campaign was a response to the Republican's very active legislative agenda in the 104th Congress (1995 through 1996). In the first hundred days of the 104th Congress, House Republicans attempted to pass various elements of their "Contract with America"—a collection of ten bills and three resolutions that dealt with issues ranging from welfare and Social Security reform to defense and military procurement.

The Contract with America's reforms were designed to slow the growth of federal spending and turn over control of many government programs to state and local governments. These proposals attempted to redefine the role of the federal government and marked a sharp departure from the federal government's activist role, which had evolved from the days of the New Deal (Gimpel 1996). The Republican reforms concerned organized labor because labor feared that state and local governments could not afford to fund social programs adequately to aid the working poor. AFL-CIO Vice President Lynda Chavez-Thompson remarked that labor's advertising campaign was a necessary measure to counter the Republican agenda. "We now have to spend [on issue ads] to bury [the Contract] six feet under" (Swoboda and Edsall 1996).

Before 1996, relatively few issue advocacy advertisements were aired. The medical and insurance industry sponsored the famous "Harry and Louise" commercial in 1994, which warned viewers of the dangers associated with President Clinton's health-care reform proposal and helped successfully turn public opinion against the plan (Goldstein 1999, 74). However, issue advocacy advertising was in its infancy as a campaign weapon in 1994 and did not become a major part of labor's election activities until Sweeney directed the advertising campaign during the 1996 elections (Magleby 2000).

Issue advocacy advertisements became an important political weapon because they exploited a loophole in federal campaign finance law. The Supreme Court ruled in *Buckley v. Valeo* (1976) that restrictions on disclosure of contributions and expenditures applied only to "express advocacy," which used "explicit words of advocacy of election or defeat" (Potter 1997, 229). By avoiding the words "vote for" or "vote against" in their advertisements, the AFL-CIO could skirt the restrictions imposed by federal campaign finance laws, namely the prohibition against using union treasury funds to pay for political advertisements. The AFL-CIO media fund was financed by $1.80 of each union member's annual dues (Swoboda and Edsall 1996).

The AFL-CIO's 1996 advertising campaign began by bringing attention to the voting records of many antilabor Republicans. In May 1996, the AFL-CIO ran issue advertisements in twenty-seven congressional districts where House members publicly opposed or voted against a minimum wage increase. The ads focused on the rise of corporate executives' salaries and the alleged hypocrisy of congressional members who voted themselves a 30 percent pay raise but refused to support a minimum wage increase, which stood at $4.25 an hour and had not been increased in five years. "We will continue to inform working families about what Congress is doing about increasing the minimum wage and how they can make their voices heard," commented Sweeney (AFL-CIO 1996c). The AFL-CIO also ran issue ads on Medicare, Social Security, and education. It targeted those ads in 105 districts with vulnerable Republicans, and spent an average of $250,000 to $300,000 in each of those districts (Beck, Taylor, Stranger, and Rivlin 1997, 11–13).

The crux of the AFL-CIO's advertising campaign, however, was to defeat potentially vulnerable antilabor Republicans in the 1996 election. To accomplish that goal, the AFL-CIO aired roughly 27,000 television commercials in forty-four districts with vulnerable House Republican incumbents (Rozell and Wilcox 1999, 140). Many of the advertisements brought attention to members' voting records on labor issues. Republican Congressman Bill Martini, of New Jersey's eighth congressional district, was one member the AFL-CIO targeted in its ad campaign. The ads criticized Martini for supporting $10 billion in student loan cuts and tax breaks for the wealthy (*The Record* 1996). The ads damaged Martini and helped his opponent, Democratic State Assemblyman and Paterson mayor Bill Pascrell, a strong union supporter, win the 1996 election by a close 51 to 48 percent margin (Barone and Ujifusa 1997, 929).

Even the few targets who won their previous election by more than twenty points found themselves in tight contests in 1996. Republican Congressman Charles Norwood of Georgia's tenth congressional district easily won election in 1994, with an impressive 65 percent of the vote. Norwood, however, found himself in a close race in 1996 against Democrat David Bell. The AFL-CIO helped Bell try to unseat Norwood with its ad campaign. One particular spot linked Norwood to House Speaker Newt Gingrich in supporting Medicare cuts and tax breaks for the wealthy (May

1996). Norwood criticized the ads, claiming they were false. He later called on Bell to "give back all the dirty labor money . . . that has the Mafia print on it" (Sherman 1996). Bell countered with attacks on Norwood's acceptance of tobacco money. In the end, Norwood escaped with a slim 52 to 48 percent victory (Barone and Ujifusa 1997, 432–433).

Other Republicans responded to the AFL-CIO media campaign by challenging the truthfulness of the advertisements. One ad about Medicare drew the ire of Republican leaders, who contended that the AFL-CIO used a quotation from Speaker Gingrich out of context. They argued the ad gave the false impression that Gingrich stated Medicare would "wither on the vine" when his remark was in reference to the Health Care Financing Administration (Toner 1996). The NRCC called the ad "defamatory" and requested that stations pull it from the air. While most stations still ran the ad, nineteen television stations and nine radio stations did not (Rozell and Wilcox 1999, 142).

More generally, Republicans charged that the AFL-CIO's ad campaign was an attempt by "union bosses" to buy the 1996 elections. "This is the first time in 40 years [the unions] haven't been in power and control. They want power and control back so they're trying to buy it," remarked Republican Congressman Dick Chrysler of Michigan, a target of the AFL-CIO issue advocacy campaign (*Congressional Quarterly* 1996, 3084). Chrysler was later defeated in his race against Democrat Debbie Stabenow after the AFL-CIO spent more than $500,000 against him (Beck, Taylor, Stranger, and Rivlin 1997, 13).

Union leaders countered that campaign expenditures by big business on behalf of Republican members were far greater than the amount spent by labor on behalf of Democrats. "It [labor money] was a drop in the bucket compared with all the money business community put into the districts where we campaigned. Business put in eight times what we put in," remarked Sweeney (Greenhouse 1996). Labor leaders also contended that their advertisements were factual and educational, and that Republican complaints were merely an attempt to avoid the truth about the voting records of GOP members. According to an AFL-CIO press release:

> The ads educate the public on both candidates' positions. The purpose of the AFL-CIO voter guide ads is to educate workers about congressional candidates' positions on issues that are central to working families' lives. The ads do not urge the viewer to either vote for or vote against either candidate. Instead, the guides lay out each candidate's position on the issue in question in a fair and even-handed manner. (AFL-CIO 1996d)

The result of the AFL-CIO campaign was the defeat of twelve of the targeted Republicans. Sweeney proudly responded after the election that the ads were "money well-spent" (Greenhouse 1996). However, Republicans were able to maintain their majority status in the U.S. House, and GOP leaders and allies were quick to dismiss the AFL-CIO's efforts as a failure. House Majority Leader Richard Armey of Texas remarked, "John Sweeney owes union members an apology for wasting their money, often against their will, only to tilt at windmills" (Greenhouse 1996). Business allies such as Bruce Josten, the senior vice president of the United States Chamber of Commerce, added: "The best answer for how labor did is to look at what Sweeney said last January, that his goal was to unseat the Republican majority. Measured against that objective, he didn't succeed" (Greeenhouse 1996).

Despite the strong rhetoric from both sides, the actual effect of the AFL-CIO's 1996 issue advocacy campaign is that it appears to have helped Democrats run stronger and more competitive campaigns in their contests against targeted Republicans (Jacobson 1999, 193). Additionally, labor's ads were a success in that they helped set the agenda on issues important to labor, such as Medicare and education (Greenhouse 1996). According to political scientist David Magleby, the AFL-CIO's issue advocacy campaign in 1996 had other important consequences. "First, labor showed other interest groups the potential power and influence that can come through successful election advocacy. Second, labor's campaign motivated political parties to raise and spend soft money, in part to counter million-dollar election-advocacy campaigns aimed at their more vulnerable incumbents and at competitive open seat races" (Magleby 2000, 47).

In early 1998, the AFL-CIO estimated that it would spend $28 million on issue advocacy advertisements. Steven Rosenthal remarked, "We plan to do issue advocacy the way we have done in the past" (O'Donnell 1998). However, labor's successful grassroots campaign in mid-1998 against Proposition 226 in California helped convince union leaders to allocate less of its resources to political advertising. The AFL-CIO ultimately spent $5 million during the 1998 elections, after concluding that the money would be better spent on grassroots work (Stranger and Rivlin 1999).

Yet despite the AFL-CIO's more limited issue-advocacy campaign in 1998, advertising was still a relevant aspect of its overall campaign efforts. In April 1997, the AFL-CIO spent roughly $700,000 on ads supporting additional funding for public schools. The ad campaign continued into 1998 and covered other policies such as free trade, the minimum wage, and the "Patient's Bill of Rights," which would allow patients to sue their HMOs for malpractice. The AFL-CIO targeted its issue ad spots mainly against Republican incumbents, and in a few instances, it ran ads critical of Democrats. In July 1997, the AFL-CIO sponsored issue ads criticizing twenty-three Republicans and seven Democrats for favoring various Republican tax proposals (Stranger and Rivlin 1999).

Union members backed the issues that the AFL-CIO covered in their 1998 ads. Some 90 percent of union members expressed approval of a Patient's Bill of Rights. Roughly 87 percent of union members supported more funding for public schools, and 85 percent believed that the federal government should use the budget surplus to strengthen Social Security (AFL-CIO 1999b).

The AFL-CIO's $5 million ad campaign in 1998 was also more expensive than those of most other political organizations (Stranger and Rivlin 1999). Labor's chief nemesis, the Coalition (a business organization comprising major groups such as the Chamber of Commerce, the National Federation of Independent Business, and the Business Leadership Council), spent just slightly more than $1 million on issue ads (Lawrence and Drinkard 1998). However, business groups used the threat of running ad campaigns against members of Congress as an effective weapon to win policy concessions. Organizations such as Americans for Tax Reform pressured several members of Congress running for reelection in 1998 to sign a pledge promising not to increase corporate taxes (Anglund and McKee 2000, 162).

Still, the AFL-CIO's advertising campaign had an effect on targeted Republican incumbents. One study found that the AFL-CIO ads decreased the share of the vote for Republicans targeted by the ad campaign by an estimated 2.9 percent when controlling for various factors (Francia 2000). In a few of the races, the small effects from the AFL-CIO's issue ads were enough to tilt the election in favor of the Democratic challenger. In the third congressional district of Kansas, for example, the AFL-CIO helped Democrat Dennis Moore, a criminal defense lawyer, defeat freshman Republican incumbent Vince Snowbarger in a very narrow election in 1998.

Snowbarger was an ideal target for the AFL-CIO. A Republican had represented the third congressional district of Kansas for almost forty years; however, the district nearly elected a Democrat in 1996. Snowbarger won a close race against Judy Hancock, 50 to 45 percent. Snowbarger was not only vulnerable, he had also built a solid reputation as a conservative and antiunion legislator in his twelve years as a Kansas state legislator and then later as member of the U.S. House in the 105th Congress. The AFL-CIO scored his labor voting record 0 percent in 1997 and just 10 percent in 1998.

Moore, on the other hand, campaigned on the same side of many issues as organized labor, championing safeguards for Social Security, endorsing the rights of patients to sue their HMOs for malpractice, and opposing school vouchers (*National Journal* 1998a, 2637). Unions supported Moore's campaign and ran several issue ads in the district attacking his opponent's voting record, particularly on Social Security.

Snowbarger charged that "labor unions were mounting a major campaign against him" (*National Journal* 1998b). His campaign responded to the AFL-CIO ads with their own commercials, which featured former presidential candidate and U.S. Senator Robert Dole. In the ad, Dole accused "big labor unions" of "distorting" Snowbarger's record on Social Security (Kurtz 1998). Dole's appearance, however, failed to save Snowbarger's campaign. Moore won a close election, receiving 52 percent of the vote to Snowbarger's 48 percent. The estimated 2.9 percent of the vote that Moore received from the AFL-CIO's campaign contributed to the outcome of this election. Indeed, the *Kansas City Star* concluded that organized labor's support was crucial to Moore's victory (Canon and Kraske 1998).

Snowbarger was not the only Republican candidate to face AFL-CIO attacks on issues such as Social Security. In Kentucky, the AFL-CIO ran issue ads against Republican Anne Northup, asking voters, "Shouldn't we save the Social Security surplus to strengthen Social Security? Most Americans say yes. But Newt Gingrich says no. And last month, Representative Anne Northup voted with Gingrich." Northup claimed the ads were false. She later countered them with ones of her own, and managed to defeat her challenger in a close race (Kurtz 1998).

Others, such as Republican incumbent Michael Pappas of New Jersey's twelfth congressional district, were not successful. Pappas, a target of AFL-CIO issue ads, lost to Democrat Rush Holt, 50 to 47 percent in 1998. Absent the 2.9 percentage point change associated with the AFL-CIO campaign, Pappas may have been able to avoid defeat. In fact, three of the five Republican defeats were by five points or less, meaning that the small effects of the AFL-CIO's media campaign may have made a large difference in races where Republicans were most vulnerable. Given the low expectations for Democrats in the 1998 elections because of the controversy surrounding Bill Clinton's impeachment scandal, and given also the intense competition for partisan control of the House, these five Democratic victories were significant. They narrowed the Republican majority in the House and increased the Democrats' chances of regaining control of the House of Representatives in 2000.

Union issue ads also were successful in influencing the issue agenda in the 1998 elections. The AFL-CIO's ad focus on Social Security, HMO reform, and education were some of the major issues that voters expressed as the most important in 1998. Social Security, health care, and education are traditionally issues that favor Democrats, and in 1998, they helped Democratic candidates attract wealthy voters and expand its base. According to one pundit, "the 1998 House campaigns moved away from GOP issues that resonate with the affluent—taxes, deficit, less government—and toward more Democratic issues—education, health care, Social Security. The effect was predictable: a significant shift in support from Republican candidates to Democratic ones" (Norman 1998, 110). Labor's ability to shape the issue agenda in 1998 through advertising played a role in helping Democrats campaign on issues on which they are traditionally strongest.

A Systematic Analysis of the AFL-CIO's Ad Campaign (2000–2002)

In 2000, the AFL-CIO spent $21.1 million on its issue ad campaign (Jamieson 2001), although many of the ads were designed to help Democratic presidential candidate Al Gore. During the final two months of the 2000 election, the AFL-CIO spent more than $1 million per week running ads in Ohio, Michigan, Missouri, and Pennsylvania critical of George W. Bush's record as governor of Texas. In the Philadelphia media market alone, the AFL-CIO spent close to $300,000 in one week on advertisements (Meckler 2000a).

Nevertheless, the AFL-CIO remained active in attempting to influence a number of congressional races with its ad campaign. In July 2000, the AFL-CIO ran advertisements in the districts of Republican House members Charles Bass of New Hampshire, Ernest Lee Fletcher of Kentucky, Don Sherwood of Pennsylvania, and James Rogan and Steven Kuykendall of California (Meckler 2000b). The AFL-CIO ad campaign, which cost about $200,000 for one week of advertisements, focused on the five Republicans' opposition to a Democratic plan that would have expanded prescription drug coverage to all seniors as part of the Medicare program. Two of the five incumbents—Rogan and Kuykendall—ultimately lost their reelection bids in 2000.

Labor again invested heavily on issue ads in 2002. In a sample of some of the most competitive races, Magleby and Monson (2003, 26) report that the AFL-CIO spent $5.6 million on advertisements, ranking only behind the United Seniors Association among interest groups. The AFL-CIO was particularly active in four incumbent-versus-incumbent races, supporting Democrats Jim Maloney of Connecticut, Tim Holden of Pennsylvania, David Phelps of Illinois, and Ronnie Shows of Mississippi (Bresnahan 2002). These efforts, however, succeeded in tipping the balance for only one of the candidates—Tim Holden, who defeated George Gekas in a close election: 51 to 49 percent.

A systematic analysis confirms that the AFL-CIO ad campaign cost Republican House incumbents a sizeable percentage of the vote in the 2000 and 2002 elections. Using advertising data from the Campaign Media Analysis Group for both election cycles, table 5.1 presents estimates generated from an OLS equation that tests the effect that the number of AFL-CIO advertisements had on House Republican incumbents' share of the vote. The results indicate that in races that had as many as 500 AFL-CIO ads (i.e., the top quartile for targeted incumbents), House Republican incumbents lost an estimated 3.5 percent of the vote (see table 5.1).

Seven Republican incumbents lost their seats in 2000 and 2002 combined. The AFL-CIO was active in most of these races, and played a decisive role in tipping the outcome in at least three of those elections. The aforementioned race involving Tim Holden and George Gekas, in the newly redrawn seventeenth congressional district in Pennsylvania, was the most expensive of the AFL-CIO's advertising campaigns. The election pitted two incumbents against each other. Holden drew strong support from several unions, including nurses, firefighters, government employees, and steelworkers. The international president of the United Steelworkers of America, Leo Gerard, stressed the importance of energizing union members and the larger Democratic base. "We can't have one Democrat that's on our side stay home," remarked Gerard. Holden himself conceded, "We've got to get our people out to vote . . . that's what it's going to come down to" (Jordan

TABLE 5.1 OLS Estimates of the Effects of AFL-CIO Advertisements on Vote Shares for Republican House Incumbents, 2000–2002

	COEFFICIENT	STANDARD ERROR
Number of AFL-CIO advertisements	–.007**	.002
Expenditure advantage over opponent (per $100,000)	.070	.067
Opponent has previous political experience	–6.713***	1.169
Partisanship of district (pro-Republican)	.525***	.051
Uncontested race	25.958***	1.811
Three or more candidates in election	–4.799***	.854
Incumbent-incumbent contest	–9.591**	4.119
Election year 2000	.550	.899
Constant	41.618***	3.115
(N)	(387)	
Adjusted R2	.62	

Note: Cases include Republican House incumbents who ran in the 1988–2002 general election. See the appendix for a complete definition of each variable.
p < .05, ** p < .01, *** p < .001.

Sources: The Campaign Media Analysis Group, the Federal Election Commission, and various editions of the *Almanac of American Politics*.

2002). To appeal to Democratic voters in the district, the AFL-CIO ran more than 200 advertisements against George Gekas and more than 400 advertisements on behalf of Holden. Several of the advertisements connected the Enron scandal to tax rebates that Gekas supported for large corporations (see figure 5.1). These advertisements appear to have helped Holden's campaign. Based on the model's estimates in table 5.1, the AFL-CIO's advertising campaign cost Gekas an estimated 4.8 percent of the vote. Holden ultimately won the election over Gekas by two points, 51 percent

"Gekas Voted With Enron"

Woman [Deborah Perotta]: " They have taken away my self-esteem. They have taken away my livelihood and they pocket my money. We, as the employees, got nothing. "

Announcer: "Enron: the symbol of corporate greed - yet Congressman George Gekas voted to give hefty tax rebates to the largest corporations, including 254 million dollars to Enron, even though Enron paid no federal taxes in four of the last five years. Tell George Gekas to invest in our schools and health care and stop rewarding corporate greed."

FIGURE 5.1 AFL-CIO Issue Advertisement in Holden-Gekas Election, 2002

Source: The Campaign Media Analysis Group.

Note: The advertisement aired from September 20, 2002, to September 21, 2002. The advertisement was paid for by the Working Men and Women of the AFL-CIO.

to 49 percent, suggesting that labor's advertising campaign played a critical role in Holden's victory.

The AFL-CIO also ran a series of ads in Senate contests. One set of ads that ran during the 2002 election was critical of Republican Senator Susan Collins of Maine. The ads against Collins focused on the senator's support of Fast Track trade authority and its alleged effect on the loss of American jobs. As one ad proclaimed, "her [Collins] job-killing votes hurt Maine" (Weinstein 2002). Collins, nevertheless, survived the ad campaign and won reelection by a convincing 58 to 42 percent against Democrat Chellie Pingree.

The AFL-CIO advertising campaign failed to show any statistically significant effect in Senate elections, although this is probably a function of the small number of races that could be analyzed for the 2000 and 2002 elections. Still, union strategists recognized the limits of their advertising campaign in the late stretches of the 2002 election. The AFL-CIO announced in mid-October that it would forgo running television advertisements in the final fifteen days of the election cycle and instead devote its resources to get-out-the-vote efforts (Bresnahan 2002). The politics of the post-9/11 terrorist attacks largely shaped the 2002 issue agenda around the war on terrorism and the possibility of war with Iraq—issues that played to the strengths of Republicans.

While the AFL-CIO made early attempts to focus the 2002 election on such issues as rising unemployment, prescription drug coverage, and Social Security, labor strategists concluded that their message was simply not getting through to voters over the airwaves. As one union official admitted, "It is proving difficult to be heard. All the talk about Iraq and terrorism may hurt [Democratic] turnout" (Bresnahan 2002). Moreover, the popularity of President George W. Bush, whose approval ratings hovered around the 70 percent mark for much of 2002, made it extremely difficult for the AFL-CIO to sell its primary message of casting blame on the president for the faltering American economy. The effect of the AFL-CIO issue advocacy advertising campaign thus appears to have produced significant results, but only in a small number of House races.

Summary

The AFL-CIO's issue advocacy campaign had some influence on House elections, although the evidence is less clear for Senate elections. Labor's advertising campaign struggled in 2002, as the post-9/11 political environment pushed issues such as the war on terrorism and the military conflict with Iraq to center stage. Yet the exceptional circumstances of the post-9/11 terrorist attacks suggest that the AFL-CIO's less effective advertising campaign in 2002 may have been only a temporary setback. Indeed, in a few House races in 2002, such as the Gekas-Holden election, the AFL-CIO ad campaign showed significant results. Given some of the AFL-CIO's success in earlier elections and its success in a few House races in 2002, a continued investment in advertising may be a strategy worth pursuing in the future.

We need to be political watchdogs, not political lapdogs. . . . as we fight for such issues as raising the minimum wage and protecting workers' health and safety, we will earn a new credibility with our members and with all working people.[1]

—JOHN SWEENEY

6

Laboring for a "Working Family" Agenda

INTEREST GROUPS HAVE one overriding purpose: to pass or protect legislation favorable to the members they represent. Unions typically assist candidates they anticipate will most likely support workers' concerns once elected to Congress. Throughout much of the 1980s and early 1990s, unions were successful in winning some elements of their legislative agenda, notably on social issues, but were unable to win legislation on high-visibility economic issues (Freeman and Medoff 1984, 192; Neustadtl 1990).

As demonstrated in the previous chapters, organized labor has strengthened its grassroots campaign operations and has played a critical role in several close elections. Yet have labor's expanded campaign efforts translated into any tangible policy victories? Have they prevented any major policy defeats? Can organized labor compete with big business when it comes to shaping public policy, and if so, what tactics are most effective?

This chapter considers those questions and assesses organized labor's strengths and weaknesses in the legislative area. The chapter begins with an overview of union lobbying techniques and compares the amount of money that unions commit to their lobbying efforts to the amounts spent by other organizations. The chapter also assesses whether organized labor's increased campaign efforts and electoral pressures have had an influence on congressional support for union policies.

Union Resources and Lobbying Techniques

Major governmental action rarely takes place without significant interest group activity. Since the founding of the American republic, interest groups have played a role in shaping virtually all major public policies. Interest groups attempt to influence policy through a process known as lobbying—a term from the nineteenth century, when group representatives would station themselves in the lobby or hallway to request favors from members of Congress.

Early lobbying efforts were sometimes little less than outright bribes. In 1852, members of Congress created a price scale for their votes, accepting money or land as payment (Greenwald 1977, 60). Lobbyists sometimes brought suitcases of cash with them to their meetings with members of Congress. Modern-day lobbying is subtler than in the past. It now relies on a variety of techniques, including testifying before Congress, hosting dinner parties and special events, and grassroots lobbying, which involves mobilizing citizens or members of the group to put pressure on members of Congress (Scholzman and Tierney 1986).

Unions influence congressional policy by relying on their economic and political resources. Economic resources refer to the methods available to labor that can affect economic events and production, such as collective bargaining, strikes, and slowdowns (Dark 1999, 36). Unions' economic resources allow them to gain access with policymakers eager to avoid disruptions in the economy.

Political resources are those methods that allow labor to influence elections directly, such as campaign contributions and expenditures, political advertising, and grassroots activities designed to mobilize union members to participate in the political process. Unions provide campaign contributions and services to shape the ideological composition of Congress by electing candidates who espouse prolabor positions. Unions also offer campaign assistance to members of Congress who serve on powerful committees. This allows unions to gain access to influential members of Congress who shape labor policies (Langbein 1986; Eismeier and Pollock 1988; Sorauf 1992). Union contributions and services may even affect congressional voting on at least some congressional roll-call votes (Kau and Rubin 1981; Kau, Keenan, and Rubin 1982; Saltzman 1987; Wilhite 1988; Burns, Francia, and Herrnson 2000), although some argue that there is not a significant relationship between campaign contributions and a legislator's roll-call votes (Wright 1985; Grenzke 1989; Wawro 2001).

Issue advertisements are often even more effective than campaign contributions. The money spent on independent advertising campaigns often exceeds union PAC contributions. The large sums of money spent on these advertising campaigns can make reelection more difficult for an incumbent. Likewise, the threat of facing a mobilized army of union volunteers is another prospect that most incumbents would rather avoid. As discussed in earlier chapters, these electoral pressures have increased in the Sweeney era, and therefore may influence congressional roll-call votes on labor legislation.

Political resources also include those that directly involve the legislative process. The AFL-CIO relies on several of its departments to assist in these efforts. Its legislative department holds issue forums and town meetings to listen to members' concerns and pursue specific policy platforms. The political department provides union members with information on pressing political issues and candidates' positions on those issues. The public policy department develops labor's specific social, economic, and trade policies. These efforts assist the AFL-CIO's lobbying activities.

Labor engages in different lobbying methods. One of its most common techniques is grassroots lobbying—a method groups use to convey the intensity of their constituents' opinions. Grassroots lobbying involves mobilizing members to put pressure on legislators and often includes massive letter and postcard campaigns. These mailings can provide useful information to voters and legislators, and can have an effect on public policies (Goldstein 1999, 126). In a May 2000 campaign, for example, steelworkers wrote more than 200,000 letters to members of Congress urging them to oppose normal trade relations with China (Greenhouse 2000b).

Labor also uses e-mail, radio, and television advertising campaigns to generate public support on a particular issue. The AFL-CIO regularly sends legislative updates through e-mail to those subscribed to its peoplepower@aflcio.org mailing list. These e-mails typically describe a problem facing the nation and instruct subscribers to contact their members of Congress. Many of the e-mails are usually laced with strong rhetoric to attract attention, and nearly always include instructions for subscribers to contact their friends, family, and coworkers (see figure 6.1).

"Put Some Coal in Tom DeLay's Stocking" (December 20, 2002)

This holiday season nearly 800,000 jobless workers lose their unemployment benefits on Dec. 28—just three days after Christmas. Their holidays will be anything but jolly because House Republican leaders, led by incoming Majority Leader Rep. Tom DeLay (R-Texas), sent Congress home for the holidays without voting on a Senate-approved measure to extend unemployment benefits.

Their outrageous failure to act means that hundreds of thousands of families already struggling without jobs now will have to scramble to put food on the table, pay mortgages or rent, and more. They join an additional million unemployed workers who earlier exhausted their benefits before finding work. This is a human and moral tragedy.

If anybody ever deserved coal in a stocking it is Tom DeLay. Take one minute right now to click on the link below and send a fax—a virtual lump of coal—to Rep. DeLay with a copy to President Bush and your representative. Tell them to restore and extend unemployment benefits as soon as Congress returns to session.

Don't forget to tell your friends, family, and coworkers about how they can put coal in Tom DeLay's stocking.

FIGURE 6.1 AFL-CIO Legislative E-Mail from Peoplepower@aflcio.org

Source: Peoplepower@aflcio.org.

To influence political policies, labor has had to rely increasingly on political resources to compensate for its weakening economic resources. In addition to its goal of electing more prounion candidates to Congress, unions also seek to use their political resources to pressure members to support their legislative agenda. As Sweeney explained, "The AFL-CIO will work to make government more accountable to working people by mobilizing in greater and greater numbers" (AFL-CIO 1999a). Its advertising campaign has a similar design. According to Deborah Dion, a spokeswoman for the AFL-CIO, labor's ad campaign helps "hold voting records under a microscope and shine a light on them" (Wolfson 1996, 40).

After Sweeney's election, the AFL-CIO made structural and organizational changes to enhance its legislative influence. One of the most significant changes involved the strengthening of its Legislative Action Committees (LACs), in order to apply more intense grassroots pressure on members of Congress. The AFL-CIO created LACs in 1981 as a pilot program. However, the Sweeney leadership uses LACs to station labor activists in swing congressional districts. These activists are responsible for meeting with congressional incumbents to discuss pending labor legislation (Heberlig 1999, 169). Moreover, LACs help educate union workers about important legislation and policies. The LACs distribute flyers that provide information to union members about how members of Congress have addressed pertinent labor issues (Heberlig 1999, 174).

Labor's Political Agenda

The primary mission of the labor movement is to improve the wages, safety, and quality of life for their members (Cornfield 1991). However, labor unions also have a long history as advocates of progressive social change (Goldfield 1987, 27). The Workingmen's parties of the mid-1800s, for example, called for a free, tax-supported public school system, abolition of imprisonment for debt, abolition of all licensed monopolies, and equal taxation on property. Local branches, such as the Workingmen's party in Philadelphia, campaigned against unsanitary and crowded housing, long working hours, and low wages (Pessen 1978). The National Labor Union, which followed the Workingmen's parties, advocated legislation for an eight-hour workday, improved workers' housing, a Department of Labor, and government management of railroads, water transportation, and the telegraph (Karson 1978). In the late 1800s, the Noble Order of the Knights of Labor pushed for workers' rights and tracked legislators' roll-call votes on labor issues (Karson 1978, 72).

Of course, organized labor has not always been on the side of progressive policies. During the late 1800s and the first half of the 1900s, the AFL opposed government-imposed wealth-redistribution policies such as unemployment insurance because it believed these benefits were best secured through collective bargaining (Hattam 1990). The AFL also supported numerous anti-immigration bills in Congress, refused to take a position against Jim Crow and lynch laws in the South, and frequently endorsed "whites only" clauses in union bylaws (Bernstein 1960, 87–88; Buhle 1999, 43–44). Nevertheless, by the time of the AFL-CIO merger in 1955, organized labor had become a public advocate for activist government programs, such as federal aid to education, better housing, medical care, and enhanced social security (Buhle 1999, 135).

The AFL-CIO of the twenty-first century has a diverse political agenda, with concerns involving trade and globalization, civil rights, public education, trade policies, immigration, health care, and workers' rights, to name just a few. Indeed, the issues covered in the AFL-CIO's recent advertising campaigns are evidence of labor's broader social concerns. In the 2000 election, for example, almost 70 percent of all AFL-CIO advertisements focused on the issue of health care (see figure 6.2). In 2002, health care was a less dominant issue, but still captured more than 30 percent of all AFL-CIO advertisements. Issues related to pension reform and free trade policies were also common—a reaction to the corporate scandals of 2002 and the congressional vote on granting "fast track" trade pact authority for President George W. Bush.

Organized labor has a broad set of concerns and clear set of issue positions on these subjects. The following sections provide a

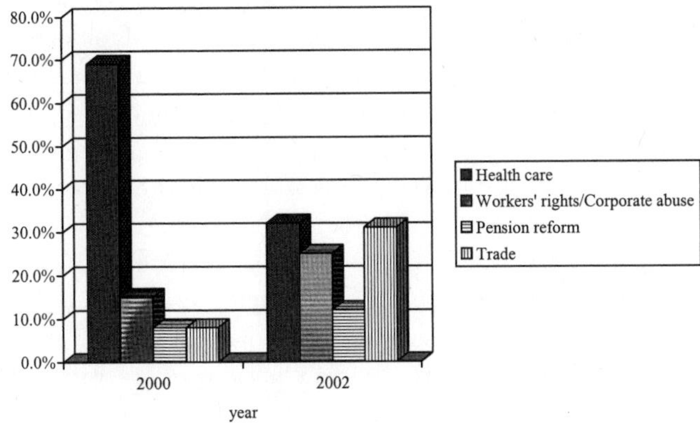

FIGURE 6.2 The Issues Covered in AFL-CIO Advertisements

Source: The Campaign Media Analysis Group.

summary of the AFL-CIO's agenda, a description of where labor stands on particular issues, and some examples of its activist and lobbying activities regarding these issues.

Free Trade and Globalization

The AFL-CIO contends that free trade and globalization policies have cost American workers their jobs and have created a downward pressure on American wages and working conditions. As the AFL-CIO notes on its website:

> Instead of bringing prosperity to workers in developed and undeveloped countries, as its proponents promised, globalization has spawned a race to the bottom where companies seek out the cheapest labor, weakest environmental laws and fewest workers' rights. As a result, millions of people in developing and developed nations work in sweatshop conditions, working long hours in unsafe and unhealthy conditions for little pay. Millions of manufacturing workers in the United States have lost good-paying jobs as plants move overseas in search of cheap labor.

Indeed, from 2001 to 2003, the United States has lost roughly 2.5 million manufacturing jobs (AFL-CIO 2003a). Manufacturing jobs have historically provided high-skilled and high-paying jobs for American workers. According to the Economic Policy Institute, the average hourly wage in 2001 for a manufacturing worker was $24.30, compared to $19.74 for workers in other service sectors (AFL-CIO 2003a).

In response, the AFL-CIO has taken several steps to address the job losses in manufacturing. It created the Industrial Union Council (IUC) to oppose free trade and other government policies that threaten American jobs or violate basic workers' rights. The AFL-CIO and affiliated unions formed the IUC in May 2002 to "revitalize manufacturing by building on the collective strength of industrial unions through joint strategies for creating and maintaining manufacturing jobs" (AFL-CIO 2003a).

The AFL-CIO also has attempted to change the rules of the global economy through its Campaign for Global Fairness. This effort has sought to empower workers' rights throughout the world. The campaign seeks to extend the right of workers to choose a union. As Sweeney explains, "We are redoubling our efforts to ensure that universally recognized core worker rights be built into the rules of the global market" (AFL-CIO 2003b).

The AFL-CIO has taken aggressive steps in the political arena to oppose congressional approval of free trade bills (Uslaner 1998). Unions have had some success in defeating several "fast track" bills, notably in 1997 and 1998 (Francia 2005). However, labor has also suffered some setbacks, such as during the 106th Congress, when the House of Representatives passed China Permanent Normal Trade Relations (PNTR). An expensive lobbying campaign by business, which some union leaders claim was as high as $50 million, and support for the pact from President Clinton helped China PNTR win passage in the House by a 237 to 197 vote (Cox 2000).

Organized labor lost another free trade vote in 2002, when Congress approved trade promotion authority for President Bush. The Republican-led House passed the bill by a narrow 215 to 212 vote that included support from 190 Republicans and twenty-five

Democrats. The opposition included 183 Democrats, twenty-seven Republicans, and two Independents (Bernard Sanders of Vermont and Virgil Goode Jr. of Virginia). A month later, the Senate passed trade promotion authority for President Bush by a 64 to 34 margin, with the support of forty-three Republicans, twenty Democrats, and one Independent.

To improve on its lobbying efforts on free trade issues, the AFL-CIO has undertaken a massive informational campaign. Unions have prompted their members to distribute fliers and have encouraged them to have their coworkers call or write their members of Congress. The AFL-CIO provides a form letter for union members to follow (see figure 6.3), but encourages members to personalize their letters by adding a paragraph of their own describing their specific concerns.

Free trade promises to be an issue that will remain a central component of labor's policy agenda. The Free Trade Area of the Americas (FTAA), which is a free trade agreement between all thirty-four countries of North America, Latin America, and the Caribbean (excluding Cuba), is just one example. The AFL-CIO has predicted that an FTAA agreement would "undermine workers' rights and environmental protections, [and] exacerbate inequality in the hemisphere" (AFL-CIO 2003b). The AFL-CIO does not reject the idea of hemispheric economic integration, but stipulates that the trade agreement must include several conditions, such as guarantees of workers' rights and protections, protection against import surges, and rules that promote "sustainable, equitable, and democratic development" (AFL-CIO 2003b). The Hemispheric Social Alliance, which includes a coalition of labor, religious, environmental, and women's and indigenous groups, led international opposition to the FTAA. The AFL-CIO has pledged to work with their international allies in opposing the FTAA, and to move this issue to the forefront of future congressional and presidential elections.

Health Care

The AFL-CIO supports health care policies that will expand health insurance coverage, although it has traditionally supported

Dear Representative/Senator:

Our nation's manufacturing sector is in crisis. The United States has lost more than two million manufacturing jobs since April 1998, accounting for 90 percent of the jobs lost in the past four years. In the past six months, every state has lost manufacturing jobs, according to the U.S. Bureau of Labor Statistics. As a share of total private nonfarm jobs, manufacturing has declined since its peak of 40 percent just after World War II to 28 percent in 1979 and now stands at 15 percent.

Our nation cannot afford to allow this decline to continue. Manufacturing is the mainstay of many states' economies and is critical to maintaining a vibrant national economy. During World War II, manufacturing built this nation's middle class. Today, manufacturing provides jobs in many sectors, including traditional industrial jobs as well as positions in communications and information technology, construction, transportation, and services.

In addition, restoring America's manufacturing base and production capacity is essential for national security in these uncertain times. We should not compromise our ability to build ships, vehicles, airplanes, machine tools, and other materials that might be vital for our nation's defense.

To rebuild our manufacturing base, I urge you to take the following urgent steps:

1. **Publicly support the freedom of workers to form unions** without employer interference, encourage workers to exercise their right to join a union, and urge employers to remain neutral during organizing campaigns.
2. **Oppose bills that would undermine worker protections**, such as "comp time" proposals that would undermine the forty-hour workweek—or the Norwood proposal to prohibit workers from organizing through voluntary card-check recognition.
3. **Support a Medicare prescription drug benefit** that provides coverage for all seniors, including those who previously were covered through employer-sponsored plans. Oppose any Medicare prescription drug proposals that discriminate against and exclude retirees who have coverage under existing employer plans.

(*continued*)

4. **Oppose any reform of the Foreign Sales Corporation (FSC) tax that would encourage the shift of more manufacturing jobs overseas.**

5. **Support legislation to stop companies from incorporating overseas** in order to avoid taxes, and deny government contracts to companies that engage in such abuses.

6. **Oppose trade agreements—including the Free Trade Area of the Americas (FTAA) currently in negotiation—that do not include meaningful protections for workers' rights** so America's industrial workers can compete fairly.

7. **Increase our national security by supporting measures to strengthen the domestic defense manufacturing base,** including procurement reform, enhanced "Buy American" requirements, and limits to "offsets" that drain critical technology and good jobs.

8. **Speak out about the crisis in manufacturing** and the need for proposals to strengthen our industrial base by initiating town hall meetings, op-ed pieces, one-minute speeches, and other outreach to the public in a timely way.

Sincerely,

FIGURE 6.3 Sample Letter from the AFL-CIO Opposing Free Trade Policies

Source: AFL-CIO. See http://www.aflcio.org/issuepolitics/manufacturing/upload/sample_congress.pdf.

accomplishing this goal through the existing employer-based system (Gottschalk 2000, 136). However, it does support policies in which the government provides prescription drug coverage for the uninsured. In 2002, the AFL-CIO ran a series of advertisements about the problems associated with the rising costs of prescription drugs (see figure 6.4).

The AFL-CIO also has fought for congressional passage of a "Patients' Bill of Rights." In 1998, the AFL-CIO backed a measure sponsored by Democratic Congressman John Dingell of Michigan and Republican Congressman Greg Ganske of Iowa that would allow patients to sue HMOs and would give doctors more power to authorize specialized care for their patients. The AFL-CIO worked together with several groups, including the American Medical Association,

"Seniors Struggling"

Man: "I take heart medication, blood pressure medication. When you just don't have the money coming in and everything's going out, you're in big trouble nowadays."

Announcer: "Our seniors are struggling, yet Congressman John Shimkus blocked a law that would have guaranteed drug coverage under Medicare. Instead, Shimkus supported a plan favored by the drug companies, which would force seniors into prescription HMOs and leave millions without coverage. Call Shimkus, tell him to stop siding with the drug companies."

Man: "The prices of prescription drugs are just killing us."

FIGURE 6.4 The Storyboard of an AFL-CIO Issue Advertisement

Source: The Campaign Media Analysis Group.

Note: The advertisement aired from August 22, 2002 to August 24, 2002. The advertisement was paid for by the Working Men and Women of the AFL-CIO.

the American Nurses Association, and the American Cancer Society to lobby members of Congress to support the bill (AFL-CIO 1998).

In July 1998, the AFL-CIO spent $1 million on radio and television advertising to win support for the legislation. One of the ads featured a Chicago nurse who said to viewers that "bureaucrats from the insurance companies . . . routinely deny care and make decisions that only doctors should be making" (Love 1998). The advertisements ran in twenty-one congressional districts and were critical of some Democrats and supportive of a few Republicans (Bresnahan 1998).

The insurance industry and business groups, which argued the bill would increase health care costs and encourage frivolous lawsuits, countered with ads of their own. The ads urged viewers to be wary of how "Washington plays doctor," and depicted Senator Edward Kennedy of Massachusetts, a sponsor of the Senate's version of the bill, as a mad scientist who creates a health care system comparable to Frankenstein's monster (Love 1998). As the airwaves flooded with ads from both sides of the issue, the AFL-CIO also worked at the grassroots level to mobilize its base. In Boston, for example, Sweeney held a "Health Care Town Meeting" to rally members about the need to reform health care, which he described a "nightmare" in the United States (Convey 1998, 25).

Despite the AFL-CIO's efforts, the Dingell-Ganske bill was ultimately defeated in a close House vote, 217 to 212. However, labor continued to push the effort in the Senate. The AFL-CIO ran television commercials opposing Senate Republicans' attempts to pass a less ambitious Patient's Bill of Rights. The ads aired in fourteen states where senators faced reelection (AFL-CIO 1998). The AFL-CIO also staged union rallies in more than thirty cities, where some members waved signs that read "Your family's health is at risk" (Solomon 1998). The bill never passed the Senate, but the AFL-CIO has pledged to continue fighting for passage of the Patient's Bill of Rights.

Jobs, Wages, Pensions, and the Economy

The AFL-CIO has been highly critical of tax cuts and policies advocated by President Bush and Republican congressional leaders. Sweeney called tax cut proposals made in the 107th Congress "morally wrong," "unwise," and "unfair," because the largest beneficiaries are the wealthiest Americans (Swoboda 2001). Labor leaders have argued that large tax cuts would jeopardize important policy priorities, including a prescription drug benefit for Medicare and shoring up the Social Security trust fund. It has pledged to fight any tax plan that does not provide low- and middle-income families with the bulk of the tax relief (Swoboda 2001).

Indeed, the issue of workers' pensions and Social Security have been important issues to organized labor for many years. The AFL-CIO strongly opposes efforts to privatize Social Security, arguing that the costs associated with such a plan would be "devastating for working families" and would lead to increases in the retirement age, cuts in guaranteed benefits, and "huge new federal deficits" (AFL-CIO 2003c). The AFL-CIO has pledged instead to defend and fight for a strengthened Social Security system.

The AFL-CIO has also consistently advocated an increase in the minimum wage. Sweeney explains:

> A job should be a bridge out of poverty, an opportunity to make a living from work. But for minimum wage workers, especially those with families, it is not. The inflation-adjusted value of the minimum wage is 24 percent lower than it was in 1979. . . . If wages had kept pace with inflation since 1968 when it was $1.60 an hour, minimum wage would be $8.46 an hour in 2003. (AFL-CIO 2003d)

The AFL-CIO has failed to win desired increases in the minimum hourly wage from $5.15 to $6.65. However, labor has succeeded in the past on this issue, as it did in 1996. Using a well-designed advertising campaign in several carefully targeted congressional districts, the AFL-CIO helped pressure members of Congress to pass a minimum hourly wage increase from $4.25 to $5.15. Nearly half of the twenty-nine Republicans targeted by the AFL-CIO ad campaign ultimately voted in favor of the minimum wage increase, contributing to its passage in the House (Francia 2005). As Sweeney noted after the bill's passage: "We [labor] were a major factor in the recent passage of the minimum wage increase. We ran extensive ads, and in the end, half the members of Congress we named in the ads voted for the increase" (AFL-CIO 1996b).

Union Lobbying

Considerable debate exists concerning organized labor's influence in shaping congressional legislation. Those who argue that unions have grown weak and ineffective in the legislative arena often cite labor's inability to overturn antiunion laws such as Taft-Hartley during periods of unified Democratic control of the federal government. Others add that unions simply cannot compete with the financial resources and the "privileged position" of business (Lindblom 1977; Vogel 1989). On the other hand, there is some evidence to suggest that unions may not be as weak in the legislative arena as the critics have suggested (Dunlop 1900; Dark 1999; Gottschalk 2000).

According to ratings published by *Fortune* magazine, the AFL-CIO was one of the top six lobbying groups in the nation from 1997 to 2001 (see table 6.1). While the AFL-CIO consistently rated ahead of the Chamber of Commerce, it trailed the National Federation of Independent Business throughout the period. The AFL-CIO also faces enormous financial disadvantages when compared to business.

Data from lobbying reports filed with the secretary of the Senate and the clerk of the House and reported by the Center for Responsive Politics indicate that from 1997 to 2000, business and other organizations outspent labor (see table 6.2). Interests representing the financial, insurance, and real estate industries were the top spenders over the four-year period, spending an average of $206 million per year. Business, labor's chief rival, spent an average of $184 million over the same period. Labor, by comparison, spent an average of just $24 million. In 2000, business outspent labor $224 million to $27 million. These dramatic financial disparities underscore the enormous disadvantages that unions must often overcome to compete with business in the legislative arena.

Unions and the Democrats

Despite the financial advantages that business has over labor, unions have depended on their close relationship with Democratic members of Congress to ward off antiunion proposals from business groups and their allies. However, several labor scholars have noted that congressional Democrats can no longer be relied upon to defend organized labor. Jeremy Brecher (1997, 345) writes that "the strategy of blaming Republicans for the labor movement's decline and looking to Democrats to reverse it [has] lost credibility." Tony Mazzocchi (1998, 247) adds, "Granted, there are a handful of Democrats out there who do their best to represent working people. But, they are hopelessly surrounded. The pro-corporate flank grows ever more militant and powerful, while the pro-worker flank shrivels, robbed of creativity and the will to fight." Yet a systematic analysis of congressional Democrats' roll-

TABLE 6.1 *Fortune*'s Top 10 Rankings of the Most Powerful Lobbying Groups

ASSOCIATION	2001	1999	1998	1997
National Rifle Association	1	2	4	6
AARP	2	1	1	1
National Federation of Independent Business	3	3	3	4
American Israel Public Affairs Committee	4	4	2	2
Association of Trial Lawyers of America	5	6	6	5
AFL-CIO	6	5	5	3
Chamber of Commerce of the U.S.A.	7	7	11	15
National Beer Wholesalers Association	8	19	24	34
National Association of Realtors	9	15	17	11
National Association of Manufacturers	10	14	13	13

Note: *Fortune* did not publish rankings for 2000.

Source: *Fortune Magazine* (editions from May 28, 2001; December 6, 1999; December 7, 1998; December 8, 1997).

call votes from the 100th Congress to the 107th Congress indicates that support from congressional Democrats on labor issues has been consistently strong.

The AFL-CIO compiles a record of each congressman's roll-call votes on union policies. These voting records, referred to as "COPE scores" (named after the AFL-CIO's Committee on Political Education), range from a high score of 100 (indicating that the member of Congress supported union policies 100 percent of the time) to a low score of 0 (indicating that the member of Congress supported union policies 0 percent of the time). The scores cover a broad range of issues, from economic policies to social welfare concerns, and are generally good indicators of bills that organized labor wishes to influence.

An analysis of these COPE scores indicates that from the 100th Congress to the 107th Congress, House Democrats consistently supported organized labor policies more than 80 percent of the

TABLE 6.2 Total Lobbyist Spending (in millions) from 1997–2000

SECTOR	AVERAGE SPENDING	1997	1998	1999	2000
Finance, Insurance, and Real Estate	$206	$177	$203	$214	$229
Miscellaneous Business	$184	$150	$169	$193	$224
Health	$184	$163	$165	$197	$209
Communications/Electronics	$184	$154	$186	$193	$201
Energy and Natural Resources	$152	$143	$149	$158	$159
Transportation	$120	$112	$115	$117	$138
Agribusiness	$92	$86	$119	$83	$78
Other	$81	$66	$69	$87	$103
Ideological/Single-Issue	$78	$73	$76	$76	$85
Defense	$53	$49	$49	$53	$60
Labor	$24	$21	$24	$24	$27
Construction	$22	$17	$22	$24	$23
Lawyers and Lobbyists	$16	$13	$19	$18	$16

Note: The column above for average spending reflects the average annual lobbyist spending from 1997 to 2000. Figures are based reports filed with the secretary of the Senate and the clerk of the House. The reports are in accordance with the Lobbying Disclosure Act of 1995. Figures were not available for 2001 and 2002 at the time of this book's completion.

Source: Center for Responsive Politics. See http://www.opensecrets.org/lobbyists/index.asp.

time (see figure 6.5). In some congresses, Democratic support for union policies averaged more than 90 percent. House Republicans, on the other hand, have grown increasingly less supportive of prolabor policies. House Republicans' COPE scores averaged 30 percent during the 100th Congress, but fell to less than 15 percent after the 104th Congress, when Republicans gained majority status in the House.

The results for the Senate follow a similar pattern. Democratic senators supported prolabor legislation more than 75 percent of the time from the 100th to the 107th Congress. The greater representation of rural, nonunion states in the Senate explains the slightly lower scores than those that exist in the House. Republican support, by contrast, ranged from an average high of 47 percent in the 100th Congress to a low of 3 percent in the 104th Congress (see figure 6.6).

These results suggest that labor's problems in the legislative arena are *not* from a lack of support from congressional Democrats. In fact, even conservative Democrats who belong to the Democratic Leadership Council recognize the importance of unions to the Democratic Party. DLC president Al From, for example, wrote in an editorial published in 1998: "I believe working Americans need a strong labor movement. . . . I will fight until the end for working Americans' right to express themselves in national politics through their labor unions . . . I believe working Americans, including those represented by organized labor, are—and always should be—a vital part of the Democratic Party" (Judis 1998, 12).

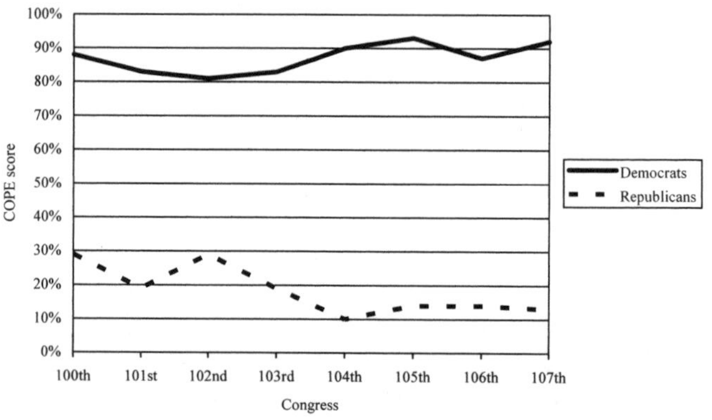

FIGURE 6.5 Average COPE Scores for House Incumbents

Source: J. Michael Sharpe, *Directory of Congressional Voting Scores and Interest Group Ratings*, 3rd ed. (CQ Press: Washington, D.C., 2000); and AFL-CIO, "Congressional Voting Record," http://www.aflcio.org/issues/legislativealert/votes/index.cfm.

Note: Cases include incumbents running for reelection.

Unions have also forged closer ties with liberal interest groups, as the divisive issues of war, race, gender, and ideology, which divided the Left in the 1970s, became less central by the late 1980s and 1990s. Organized labor worked closely with civil rights groups in the 101st and 102nd Congresses on the Civil Rights Act, and formed alliances with environmentalists on numerous free trade bills throughout the 1990s. These broader partnerships with the progressive community have helped labor put added pressure on congressional Democrats. The Democrats, in turn, have responded to these pressures, and as the results demonstrate, have largely supported labor's agenda.

Labor's policy difficulties are instead the result of its inability to forge any semblance of a coalition with moderate Republicans in the House and Senate. During the 102nd Congress—one of the last sessions of Democratic control of the U.S. House—the Democrats passed a bill to outlaw the permanent replacement of striking

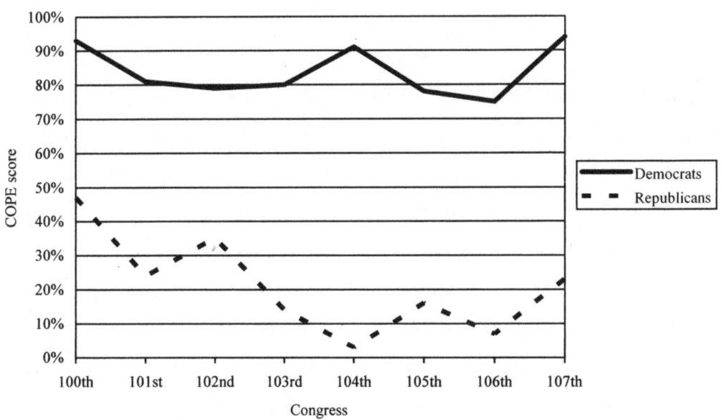

FIGURE 6.6 Average COPE Scores for Senate Incumbents

Source: J. Michael Sharpe, *Directory of Congressional Voting Scores and Interest Group Ratings*, 3rd ed. (CQ Press: Washington, D.C., 2000); and AFL-CIO, "Congressional Voting Record," http://www.aflcio.org/issues/legislativealert/votes/index.cfm.

Note: Cases include incumbents running for reelection.

workers by an overwhelming margin of 247 to 182. The bill, however, died in the U.S. Senate because of a Republican-led filibuster. Fifty-two out of fifty-seven Senate Democrats supported the bill—roughly 91 percent of Senate Democrats. On the other hand, just five of forty-three Republicans supported the bill—roughly 12 percent of Senate Republicans. This committed Republican opposition was enough to stop the bill from passing Congress.

Election Pressures, Union Density, and Labor Legislation

As the previous results have demonstrated, unions generally receive strong support from congressional Democrats on labor policies. One reason that may explain this is that Democrats are likely to be predisposed to support union policies. On the other hand, it seems plausible that labor's campaign contributions and expenditures may play some role in influencing Democrats to support union policies (see, e.g., Saltzman 1987). Likewise, Democrats who receive corporate contributions may feel pressure to support policies that the business community favors but that organized labor opposes (Eismeier and Pollock 1988). Corporate contributions are likely to serve as a cross-pressure for Democrats, and may mitigate the effects of union expenditures and contributions.

Constituent pressures are also likely to affect congressional members' policy positions. Members who represent districts in regions with the most union members are likely to be the most susceptible to supporting prolabor policies. Specifically, Democratic members of Congress in areas with the highest percentage of union workers should face the most pressure to support prounion policies and should be the most likely to support prolabor policies.

Electoral pressures are another factor that could shape congressional Democrats' roll-call votes on labor issues. Democrats in safe districts often build close ties with unions because organized labor desires access to likely winners (Dark 1999). These members are often more inclined to support labor policies (Saltzman 1987).

The effects of these many factors on Democrats' support for union policies are considered in the next section. However, because members of Congress who receive contributions and assistance from political organizations may be predisposed to support that group's interests, the direction of causality is unclear. Union contributions and expenditures may influence congressional support for labor legislation, but unions are also likely to reward the congressmen who support their agenda (Wright 1996).

As a consequence, traditional estimation procedures such as ordinary least squares (OLS) regression can overstate the effects of contributions and campaign assistance on member support for the group's interests (Chappell 1981; 1982). The two-stage-least-squares (2SLS) method is the most widely accepted technique to correct for this problem. Because the data are from more than one time period, the analysis that follows relies on generalized two-stage-least-squares (G2SLS). (For a further discussion on G2SLS, see Achen 1986.) Union campaign contributions and expenditures and the member's support for union legislation (measured based on COPE scores) serve as the endogenous variables. (See the appendix for a definition of how each measure was operationalized and for information on the statistical analysis and estimation.)

Labor Support from House Members

The results in table 6.3 indicate that as House Democrats received more union campaign assistance, their support for labor policies increased. For every $100,000 received in union contributions and expenditures, support for labor legislation increased roughly 2.8 percentage points among House Democrats. However, the results also suggest that House Democrats became less supportive of labor as their assistance from corporate PACs increased. For every $100,000 received in corporate contributions and expenditures, support for labor legislation decreased by roughly 2.4 percent among House Democrats.

During the Kirkland period, unions contributed and spent an average of $110,294 (in 2002 dollars) on House Democrats. However, corporate PACs contributed and spent $105,771 of their own on House Democrats, mitigating any prounion legislative effect. The results were similar during the Sweeney period,

TABLE 6.3 G2SLS Estimates of the Effects of Campaign and Constituency Factors on House Democrats' Support for Labor Policies, 100st Congress Through 107th Congress

	COEFFICIENT	STANDARD ERROR
+Union expenditures and contributions (per $10,000)	.278*	.133
Corporate expenditures and contributions (per $10,000)	–.243***	.046
Union density	.596***	.094
Competitive district	–2.611***	.816
Constant	75.861***	1.612
(N)	(1,651)	
Adjusted R-Square	.27	

Note: All expenditures are indexed for inflation to reflect 2002 dollars. Cases include House incumbents who ran for reelection in the 1988–2002 general election. The "+" denotes the instrumented variable.
* $p < .05$, ** $p < .01$, *** $p < .001$.

Sources: Information on AFL-CIO scores came from J. Michael Sharpe, *Directory of Congressional Voting Scores and Interest Group Ratings*, 3rd ed. (CQ Press: Washington, D.C., 2000); and AFL-CIO, "Congressional Voting Record," http://www.aflcio.org/issues/legislativealert/votes/index.cfm. Campaign finance and election data came from the Federal Election Commission. Information on union density came from Barry T. Hirsch, David A. Macpherson, and Wayne G. Vroman, "Estimates of Union Density by State," *Monthly Labor Review* 124, no. 7 (July 2001): 51–55.

with unions contributing and spending an average of $106,890 and corporate PACs contributing and spending $99,472.

While corporate contributions and expenditures have limited the effect of union campaign contributions and expenditures in influencing House Democrats' support for labor legislation in both the Kirkland and Sweeney periods, organized labor's efforts to organize more workers may be the more effective strategy for winning legislative battles in Congress. A ten-point increase in the percentage of union workers in a congressman's state (roughly the difference between Colorado and Illinois) increases support for labor legislation among House Democrats by almost 6 percentage points. Organizing more union workers is important because it increases constituent pressures on House Democrats to support union policies, which subsequently can have an effect on labor policies.

The results also indicate that House Democrats in the safest seats were the most likely to support labor policies. Many of these "safe" members build seniority and win positions on important and powerful congressional committees. This suggests that unions have the support of some of the more influential Democrats in Congress.

A comparable analysis for House Republicans also demonstrates that union assistance can translate into increased labor support (see table 6.4). For every $10,000 in union contributions and expenditures, House Republican support for labor issues increases by 1.5 percent. Union density is also significantly related to House Republicans' support for labor policies. House Republicans' support for union issues increases by more than one percentage point for each percentage point increase in union density. This reinforces the conclusion that organizing more union workers is a critical component to building a labor movement that is more influential in the legislative process.

It is more difficult to draw conclusions about labor's influence in the U.S. Senate. Senate elections occur every six years and only a small number of incumbents seek reelection, making it difficult to perform a meaningful systematic analysis of how labor assistance affects Senate support for labor policies. The correlation for Senate Democrats' COPE scores and union assistance is quite weak (r = .20). Among Senate Republicans, there is a strong correlation (r = .65), but few Senate Republicans receive any meaningful labor assistance.

Union density, on the other hand, is an important variable for both Senate Democrats and Republicans. The correlation for Senate Democrats' COPE scores and union density is fairly strong (r = .40). Among Senate Republicans, the correlation is higher (r = .51). In sum, the Senate results confirm that increasing the percentage of union workers in a constituency is likely to have an important effect on roll-call votes in the Senate that

TABLE 6.4 G2SLS Estimates of the Effects of Campaign and Constituency Factors on House Republicans' Support for Labor Policies, 100st Congress Through 107th Congress

	COEFFICIENT	STANDARD ERROR
+Corporate expenditures and contributions (per $10,000)	–.009	.185
Union expenditures and contributions (per $10,000)	1.571***	.227
Union density	1.017***	.103
Competitive district	–.285	1.206
Constant	.900	3.489
(N)	(1,403)	
Adjusted R-Square	.26	

Note: All expenditures are indexed for inflation to reflect 2002 dollars. Cases include Senate incumbents who ran for reelection in the 1988–2002 general election. The "+" denotes the instrumented variable.

* $p < .05$, ** $p < .01$, *** $p < .001$.

Sources: Information on AFL-CIO scores came from J. Michael Sharpe, *Directory of Congressional Voting Scores and Interest Group Ratings*, 3rd ed. (CQ Press: Washington, D.C., 2000); and AFL-CIO, "Congressional Voting Record," http://www.aflcio.org/issues/legislativealert/votes/index.cfm. Campaign finance and election data came from the Federal Election Commission. Information on union density came from Barry T. Hirsch, David A. Macpherson, and Wayne G. Vroman, "Estimates of Union Density by State," *Monthly Labor Review* 124, no. 7 (July 2001): 51–55.

pertain to labor issues. Strengthening the political power of organized labor in the legislative arena is thus likely to hinge on its ability to organize more workers.

Summary

Organizing more union workers is a point that cannot be stressed enough. As chapter 4 demonstrated, union workers provide labor with the manpower to counter the financial power of business in congressional elections. Likewise, labor can apply effective pressure on congressmen and senators to support prounion policies when there are sufficient numbers of union workers in the district or state.

Of course, while the evidence suggests that organizing more workers is necessary for unions to strengthen their position in congressional politics, this solution is certainly easier said than done. On the one hand, unions need a sympathetic Congress to ease restrictions on organizing. And on the other hand, unions need to organize more workers to elect a sympathetic Congress. Solving this "chicken or the egg" dilemma does not have any easy answers. However, a good beginning to solving the problem would be for all local unions to invest at least 30 percent of their budgets into organizing, as Sweeney has recommended. Indeed, several major unions including the SEIU and UNITE HERE have invested 50 percent of their budgets into organizing (Benz 2004). Not surprisingly, these unions have had the most success in organizing workers. Sweeney must continue to insist that local unions commit more of their resources to organizing. While organizing workers is often thought of in terms of its economic effects (e.g., the average salaries of union workers versus nonunion workers, job creation, etc.), its political effect is equally significant. The future of organized labor in congressional politics will likely depend on its ability to organize.

The results of this chapter also make clear that labor's problem lies not with congressional Democrats but with the increasing hostility of congressional Republicans toward unions. For unions to succeed in the policy arena, they will not only need to organize more workers, but they will also need to use whatever strength they have from their current membership to elect more Democrats or to make better efforts to win support from moderate Republicans.

The history of American workers has not been a story of progressive ascent from oppression to securely established rights, nor has it offered us a past moment of democratic promise that was irretrievably snuffed out by the consolidation of modern capitalism. Their movement has grown only sporadically and through fierce struggles, been interrupted time and again just when it seemed to reach flood tide, overwhelmed its foes only to see them revive in new and more formidable shapes, and been forced to reassess what it thought it had already accomplished and begin again.[1]

—DAVID MONTGOMERY, YALE UNIVERSITY, PROFESSOR OF HISTORY

7

Conclusion

The Significance of Union Renewal

THE DECLINE OF organized labor in the United States, particularly in the political arena, seemed a foregone conclusion during the mid-1990s, following the Republicans' takeover of the U.S. Congress. Unions faced a hostile Congress for the first time in four decades and simply could not compete dollar for dollar with their opponents in the business community. Union PACs, which allocated more money in congressional elections than corporate PACs in the late 1970s, were outspent by corporate PACs in the 1994 election by a four-to-one ratio. Organized labor's membership, long its most important political resource, fell as a percentage of the workforce throughout the 1980s and 1990s. Of the union members that remained, the labor movement often failed to mobilize them politically. Organized labor seemed to be at a point in its history where, as David Montgomery described, it needed to reassess what it thought it had already accomplished and begin anew.

The election of John Sweeney as president of the AFL-CIO in 1995 marked an important turning point for organized labor. While some scholars have been skeptical of whether Sweeney has provided genuine reform and has been able to begin rebuilding the labor movement, the evidence presented in this book indicates otherwise. Sweeney has made some significant changes in the AFL-CIO's political activities and strategies. Perhaps the most important change has been to expand labor's political efforts beyond merely writing checks. Since Sweeney's election, organized labor has waged an extensive air and ground war in congressional elections.

These efforts have had several important consequences. Labor's grassroots efforts have increased union members' political participation. Union households have consistently been a larger segment of the electorate during the Sweeney era than they were during the Kirkland era, despite declines in union membership as a percentage of the workforce. Members of union households also have maintained their strong support for Democratic candidates, despite rising support for Republican candidates in nonunion households.

Organized labor's increased grassroots and independent expenditures, as well as its issue advocacy advertisements, have also helped Democratic congressional candidates wage stronger campaigns. Labor's campaign efforts have been particularly successful during the Sweeney era in both House and Senate elections. Skeptics of labor's success during the Sweeney era will undoubtedly point to the fact that Republicans have maintained their majority status in the House and Senate for most of Sweeney's tenure. However, the findings in this study make clear that Democrats would have won even fewer seats in Congress were it not for the changes to labor's strategies during the Sweeney era.

The evidence is more mixed, however, concerning labor's success in the legislative area. Labor's best hope to make gains in the legislative process will be to organize more workers. Congressmen and senators respond to pressure from their constituents. Unions need manpower to win policy battles against business, and will need to reverse the declines in their membership as a percentage of the workforce if they hope to strengthen their legislative influence.

If unions cannot make tangible gains in increasing their membership, then they will need to hope for a resurgence of the Democratic Party in congressional elections. House Democrats in the most recent Congresses have supported unions on more than 90 percent of their issues. The most prominent congressional leaders in the Democratic party, House Minority Leader Nancy Pelosi and former Senate Minority Leader Thomas Daschle each have career labor records of 96 percent and 85 percent respectively. The Democrats' previous House leadership, Richard Gephardt and David Bonior, were consistent supporters of prolabor policies. Both Gephardt and Bonior recorded lifetime labor scores of 88 percent and 96 percent respectively. By comparison, the current Republican House leadership, Dennis Hastert and Tom DeLay, have career labor records of 7 and 2 percent respectively.

Of course, assigning blame to congressional Republicans for labor's policy failures gives little comfort to those seeking to advance workers' rights, especially during a time when Republicans appear increasingly likely to embrace the policies of its strongly conservative wing. Republicans have maintained their majorities, and may continue to control Congress for years to come. At a minimum, Republicans should easily be able to maintain a large enough bloc in the U.S. Senate to thwart any major labor policies or reforms. On the other hand, organized labor's improved ability to assist in the election efforts of congressional Democrats should allow it to thwart any attacks made against unions and workers by congressional Republicans. However, unions certainly should aspire to more than simply maintaining the status quo. The question then becomes: How should organized labor proceed in advancing its agenda in the twenty-first century?

Advancing Labor's Cause

The formation of a "labor" political party is one of the most common suggestions for advancing labor's cause. Several labor scholars contend that organized labor will only regain its political strength by divorcing itself from the Democratic Party and supporting third parties, such as the New Party or the Labor Party (Brecher and Costello 1998, 16; Buhle 1999; Lichtenstein 1998; Slaughter 1999, 52). However, this idea faces the obstacles that minor parties must confront in the United States.

First, the winner-take-all structure of the American election system makes it extremely difficult for third parties to win seats. Second, there are legal barriers such as ballot access laws that require most minor-party candidates to circulate petitions and obtain several thousand signatures from citizens in their district to have their name appear on the ballot. Third, minor-party candidates must also contend with the fact that voters are socialized to accept the two-party system norm (Rosenstone, Behr, and Lazarus 1996). Citizens realize the long odds of winning office faced by minor-party candidates and are often inclined to avoid "throwing their vote away." The strategic considerations of voters make it extremely difficult for minor-party candidates to win over supporters (Riker 1982).

Indeed, from 1988 to 2002, all minor-party candidates, including independents, averaged just 5 percent of the vote in congressional elections.[2] Even when labor formed the Workingmen's Party during the early and mid-1800s, their issues were simply coopted by the Democratic Party. For these reasons, the third-party option is simply not viable for organized labor to pursue if it is serious about strengthening its political influence.

Other more radical proposals include calls for workers to look to socialism. As Kim Moody (1997, 310) writes, "Those [workers] who are simply looking for a better life would do well to look to a socialist movement for hope." Yet union workers in the United States have long rejected socialist influences, and there is simply no indication that this is likely to change. As Harry Katz (2001, 341) observes, "There is much evidence that workers have borne the burden of layoffs and economic insecurity over the last twenty years, yet there is scant evidence that this has led these workers to seek radical political change." Moreover, when the working class is sufficiently mobilized, unions have had some significant political victories under capitalism, such as the passage of the National Labor Relations Act (Gerstle 2002, 332).

Instead of proposals that have little chance of becoming reality, the American labor movement needs practical suggestions that will allow them to make progress in the existing capitalist, two-party system. For those in the labor movement who remain unconvinced that congressional Democrats have served unions well, there remains the viable option of the primary election to replace disloyal Democrats. This is a strategy that organized labor has already used effectively in recent elections. As discussed in chapter 2, unions mobilized to defeat two Democratic incumbents, Marty Martinez of California and Tom Sawyer in Ohio, because of their support for free trade policies. Hilda Solis and Tim Ryan, the victors of those two primaries respectively, have been two of the most reliable supporters of prounion policies since their election. Solis has supported organized labor on all of their policy issues.

Indeed, the wisdom of involvement in primary elections has been followed with success by other progressive forces in the Democratic Party. For the better part of the last three decades, organizations committed to expanding female and minority representation in Congress have recruited candidates to run in Democratic primaries. When women and racial minorities have gone on to win election to Congress, they did so not by forming their own political party, but by building progressive coalitions and mobilizing these forces within the Democratic Party. Unions certainly can and should follow this model to improve their representation in Congress.

Organized labor should also support a larger number of moderate Republicans in *safe* districts than it currently does. Of course, many moderate Republicans are not in safe districts. In these instances, the choice is more difficult. Democratic candidates are almost always likely to be more supportive of labor's agenda than moderate Republicans, and union interests are better served when Democrats are in control of Congress. For these reasons, labor's ability to build a relationship with moderate Republicans is somewhat limited. However, there are several moderate Republicans in relatively safe districts, such as Congressman Jack Quinn of New York. Quinn has welcomed labor's support and has noted that it represents "a step in the right direction" toward encouraging additional GOP members to support union issues (VandeHei 1998). Supporting moderate Republicans would allow unions the ability to forge cross-party coalitions capable of building the majorities necessary to pass legislation. With Congress so evenly divided between Democrats and Republicans, moderate "swing" members in the House and Senate are often the decisive votes that determine the difference between victory and defeat of a bill. As Quinn himself has observed, "I think [union leaders] have discovered that in a chamber where there is a five-, six- or seven-vote majority, there are some moderate Republicans who can make the difference" (Cochran and Adams 2001, 2005).

Prolabor Republicans, as members of the majority party, are also more likely than Democrats to convince committee and subcommittee chairs to moderate legislative language on a labor bill. They would have more influence with the Rules Committee, which can provide opportunities to present prolabor amendments to the floor. In the Senate, only a few prolabor Republicans, by supporting filibusters, are needed to thwart conservative attempts to pass antiunion legislation.

Indeed, cross-party coalitions can succeed in the policy arena. Despite Democratic control of Congress, the "conservative coalition" of Republicans and southern Democrats allowed conservatives to thwart progressive policies in the Congress and even pass conservative policies, such as the 1981 Reagan tax cuts. A coalition of Democrats and moderate Republicans from states in the Northeast, Midwest, and West could form the voting bloc in Congress that unions need to protect and perhaps eventually expand workers' rights. Labor should support moderate Republicans if for no other reason than to halt the continuing ideological drift of the Republican Party toward its more extreme conservative wing.

The Outlook for Organized Labor in American Politics

Despite some discouraging trends such as the declines in union density, there are several positive developments for organized labor. First, demographic changes in the United States provide potential for progressives to become a stronger force in American politics (Judis and Texeira 2002). These changes may foster a more favorable climate for unions. With rising numbers of Latino immigrants entering the United States, organized labor's overtures to welcome and embrace these workers could help future organizing efforts. The AFL-CIO's reversal of its historic opposition to immigrant workers offers new potential for unions to replenish their diminishing ranks and to expand their political influence through the Latino community, as they have already done successfully in cities such as Los Angeles. The AFL-CIO's more inclusive philosophy has also extended to college students, environmentalists, and civil rights activists. Rather than acting as a divisive influence, as the AFL-CIO did in 1972 when it refused to join progressives in support of Democratic presidential nominee George McGovern, the AFL-CIO, beginning with its Project '96 campaign, has cooperated and formed alliances with other groups in the progressive community. New organizations, such as Americans Coming Together, Grassroots Democrats, and America Votes, are further evidence of these strengthened ties.

Of course, numerous obstacles remain for organized labor. The continuing decline of union membership as a percentage of the workforce is a problem. Expanding the union ranks, particularly in the southern United States where union density is lowest, must be a top priority for the AFL-CIO in coming years. In addition to the need for local unions to allocate at least 30 percent of their budgets to organizing, even more can and should be done. The AFL-CIO should also aggressively challenge "right-to-work" laws. Organizing campaigns are a tough sell to workers in these states because of the so-called "free rider" problem. Workers who choose not join the union still enjoy the benefits won by other union workers, but do so without the costs associated with union membership. However, organized labor can combat that problem by publicizing some of the advantages of joining a union. For example, a union worker's average hourly earnings is $21.45, compared to $16.96 for nonunion workers (Bureau of Labor Statistics 2004a), and 89 percent of union workers receive medical care benefits, compared to 67 percent of nonunion workers (Bureau of Labor Statistics 2004b). The AFL-CIO certainly has plenty of ammunition to wage an effective campaign.

In addition, the AFL-CIO could improve its organizing success by borrowing from its own political strategies. The AFL-CIO's "people-powered politics" relies on member-to-member communications. The same model could be applied to organizing campaigns. Union members, rather than paid staff, should help carry the message to unorganized workers about the benefits of belonging to a union. Union workers best understand the fears that nonunion workers face about joining a union because they once experienced the same anxieties.

Organized labor must also look to organize and expand workers' rights worldwide. In an era of economic globalism, where corporations routinely flee industrialized countries with worker protection laws and relocate in third-world nations to take advantage of the laissez-faire business environment, organized labor must become a global force of its own. Millions of workers continue to toil in slavelike conditions throughout the world, and desperately need a voice to fight for their interests. Fighting for workers' rights abroad is not only a moral imperative, but will also save union jobs in the United States and allow organized labor the opportunity to once again grow in size, enhancing its political power.

Of course, organizing more workers, particularly abroad, but even in the United States, will be a daunting challenge. While there is some evidence that union growth can occur quickly and in spurts, organizing is more likely to be a long-term strategy that will probably take decades to effect meaningful change. Unions have successfully enlisted several congressional Democrats to help their cause. In July 2002, Democratic Congressman James McGovern of Massachusetts sent a pointed letter to employees at the Saint-Gobain Abrasives factory, criticizing the company's efforts to thwart an organizing drive by the UAW. McGovern noted in the letter that "if it were me, I'd vote to unionize." Several days later, workers voted 406 to 386 in favor of unionizing, prompting organizer Richard Bensinger to comment, "we would not have won if he [McGovern] hadn't done it" (Moberg 2002, 19). Indeed, with Republicans in control of Congress, organized labor has focused less of its efforts on trying to win support for the reform of organizing laws, and instead has directed its energy into persuading members of Congress, particularly Democrats, to support organizing drives back in their home districts (Heberlig 1999, 175).

Organizing has indeed become the hot subject in the labor

movement. Sweeney has faced vocal criticism from within the labor movement about the need to consider even bolder steps to organize more workers. Andrew Stern, who heads the SEIU, helped form the New Unity Partnership in 2003. The NUP has proposed that the AFL-CIO combine its sixty affiliated unions into fifteen or twenty "megaunions," to create a larger collective unit with greater bargaining power (Bernstein 2004). The AFL-CIO should seriously consider such sweeping proposals. If Sweeney ignores these calls or fails to rise to the challenge of organizing more workers, he may face a serious challenge to his leadership.

While organizing efforts unfold, unions will need to make the most of the members and the resources that they currently have. Many workers, blue- and white-collar alike, are frustrated and angry about the shrinking American paycheck and lack of job security. Labor leaders need to tap into that anger as a means to focus and mobilize working-class Americans to defend their interests, particularly in an era dominated by rampant and arrogant corporate greed, as exemplified by the Enron, WorldCom, Adelphia Communications, Tyco, and Global Crossing scandals of 2002. Sweeney's "America Needs a Raise" campaign was a good beginning in this respect, and the AFL-CIO's "Eye on Corporate America," is another step in the right direction. Organized labor should continue these and similar efforts in the future.

In the electoral arena, organized labor should continue its commitment to grassroots political mobilization and issue advocacy advertisements. Both efforts have yielded significant results for organized labor in congressional elections. They have also helped maintain labor's strong alliance with congressional Democrats.

Innovative leadership will also remain critical to the strength of the labor movement. While Salisbury's "exchange theory" teaches that leaders need to provide benefits for their members in the form of material, solidary, or purposive benefits, and Olson points to the importance of leaders providing "selective benefits," this study demonstrates the primary role that leaders can play in empowering rank-and-file members. As the example of John Sweeney and the AFL-CIO illustrates, when leaders make serious efforts to mobilize their membership, they can revitalize their organizations and even counter the efforts of wealthier groups. Business regularly outspends all other groups, but it is not always successful because of its difficulties in organizing a unified front. Money does matter in politics, but as labor has demonstrated under Sweeney, groups with less money can often overcome financial disadvantages through well-organized grassroots efforts and better organization, strategy, and allocation of resources.

The results in this study also confirm the importance of campaign efforts in elections. Put simply, the campaign efforts of interest groups matter in elections. This may seem an obvious conclusion to real-life political practitioners, campaign managers, and candidates. However, it is a point worth reemphasizing to political scientists who for too long have downplayed the importance of campaign effects in elections. Indeed, the evidence in this book makes clear that without the campaign efforts of organized labor, many Democratic congressional candidates would have lost elections that they otherwise won. This is not to suggest that unions are completely responsible for the successes or failures of Democratic candidates. In fact, union efforts only matter in a small number of very competitive races. However, the campaign efforts of organized labor can make a difference in these marginal but critically important contests that can ultimately determine which party governs.

Thus, for unions to succeed and survive in the twenty-first century, the leadership of the AFL-CIO will need to avoid the complacency of the past. There is a great deal at stake. A labor movement that withers will likely trigger only greater disparities in the nation's distribution of wealth—a situation that is already quite grave. The average chief executive now earns between 300 to 400 times the salary of the average worker (Johnson 1999). A worker earning a typical annual salary of $35,000 would need to work almost three millennia—roughly 2,857 years—to equal the compensation of a CEO earning $100 million a year. Moreover, while working hours have fallen in nearly all industrial nations of the world, American workers have seen their work time increase, and now work more hours per year than workers in any other of the world's industrial nations. This means less time for parents to spend with their children, less time for people to interact and socialize in their communities, and less time for people to devote to even a modicum of leisure.

Without a strong labor movement—particularly in the political arena—who or what will be left to defend the interests of workers against corporations and big business? Who or what will provide the collective voice of workers to express their concerns to government officials? As the leaders of the AFL-CIO set organized labor's course for the twenty-first century, their decisions will not only have consequences for the future of organized labor in American politics, but the type of society that evolves over the next century in the United States. As John Lewis once said, "the future of labor is the future of America."

This is the most critical election in the long history of the American labor movement.[1]

—JOHN SWEENEY

8

Postscript

The 2004 Election

THE 2004 ELECTION witnessed one of the largest political efforts that organized labor has ever assembled. As Sweeney explained in March 2004, "America's unions are united for the biggest and earliest mobilization effort for the 2004 elections in the union movement's history" (Greenhouse 2004). The AFL-CIO pledged to spend $44 million in a campaign aimed primarily at defeating President George W. Bush, but also designed to assist Democrats in regaining control of Congress.

However, organized labor had to shift its strategies in 2004 because of changes in federal campaign finance law. The 2004 election was the first under regulations specified in the Bipartisan Campaign Reform Act (BCRA). Since Sweeney's election, the AFL-CIO had been a significant "soft" money contributor to Democratic Party committees. However, with the enactment of BCRA, organized labor needed to redirect its money to other channels, because the new law banned national party committees from soliciting soft money contributions.

Labor responded to changes in the campaign environment during the 2004 election; however, the results were a major disappointment for labor, given its failed efforts to elect Democratic nominee John Kerry to the White House and to elect Democratic majorities to the Congress. The 2004 election results would seem to suggest that unions may have lost much of the strength and influence in electoral politics that this book purports the labor movement has regained under the Sweeney leadership. However, a close examination of the data from the 2004 election indicates that Democrats did not fail to win the White House or regain control of Congress because of labor.

Labor's Political Efforts in 2004

The AFL-CIO was very active in the 2004 election. The AFL-CIO sent out more than thirty million pieces of mail to union households. Union volunteers distributed a total of thirty-two million leaflets, knocked on six million doors, and contacted more than 90 percent of all union members (AFL-CIO 2004).

In the competitive "battleground" states, 92 percent of union members received a union pamphlet, flyer, or letter during the election, 88 percent received a union newspaper, magazine, or newsletter, and 66 percent received a telephone call from the union (Hart Research Associates 2004). There were more than 5,500 full-time staff or union members in these battleground states—a significant increase from the 1,500 full-time staff in 2000. Union members from nonbattleground states, including California, New York, New Jersey, and Massachusetts, even traveled to swing states to mobilize the union vote (AFL-CIO 2004).

These efforts contributed to a large union turnout in the 2004 election. Union households accounted for 27 million voters or 24 percent of the electorate in 2004 (Gruenberg 2004). Voters from union households supported Democratic presidential nominee John Kerry by a margin of 65 percent to 33 percent over President Bush (see table 8.1). The margin for Democrats was even greater in U.S. House elections. Roughly 69 percent of union-household voters supported a Democratic House candidate, compared to the 29 percent supporting a Republican House candidate. Given the large turnout of voters from union households

TABLE 8.1 Union Households in the 2004 Election

	DEMOCRAT	REPUBLICAN	OTHER
President	65%	33%	2%
U.S. House	69%	29%	2%
N = 1,135			

Source: Peter Hart Research Associates, AFL-CIO Election Night Survey, Study #7454, November 2, 2004.

and their disproportionate support for John Kerry and House Democrats, labor unions certainly did their part to assist Democrats in the 2004 election.

Unions also did their part in educating their members to support a progressive political agenda. On health-care issues, roughly four out of every five people from union households strongly favored guaranteeing health coverage for all children and giving Medicare the power to negotiate with drug companies to reduce drug costs for seniors (see table 8.2). Large majorities of members from union households also favored allowing the importation of prescription drugs from Canada and expanding access to health care for the uninsured.

On economic issues, 70 percent of members from union households strongly favored strengthening protections for a worker's right to join and form a labor union. Some 72 percent strongly supported reforming trade agreements to include protections for workers' rights and human rights. Some two-thirds strongly favored raising the minimum wage to $7.00 an hour and closing tax loopholes that encourage American companies to send jobs overseas. A majority strongly favored repealing the Bush tax cuts for the wealthiest one percent, and strongly opposed efforts to privatize Social Security.

The political attitudes of members from union households certainly put them on the side of most Democrats. This reinforces the point that the Republicans' success in the 2004 election seems to have little to do with any failure on the part of organized labor.

TABLE 8.2 Political Attitudes in Union Households, 2004

	STRONGLY FAVOR	SOMEWHAT FAVOR	SOMEWHAT OPPOSE	STRONGLY OPPOSE	NOT SURE
Guaranteeing health coverage for all children	80%	12%	4%	2%	2%
Giving Medicare the power to negotiate with drug companies to reduce drug costs for seniors	77%	15%	1%	3%	4%
Allow the importation of prescription drugs from Canada	64%	22%	5%	5%	4%
Expanding access to health care for those who are currently uninsured	62%	23%	4%	5%	6%
Strengthening protections for workers' right to join and form labor unions	70%	21%	3%	3%	3%
Reforming trade agreements to include protections for workers' rights and human rights	72%	18%	2%	2%	6%
Raising the minimum wage to $7.00 an hour	67%	17%	5%	8%	3%
Closing tax loopholes that encourage U.S. companies to send jobs overseas	67%	9%	4%	17%	3%
Repealing the Bush tax cuts for the wealthiestone percent	57%	8%	7%	24%	4%
Privatizing Social Security	12%	12%	9%	55%	12%
N = 1,135					

Source: Peter Hart Research Associates, AFL-CIO Election Night Survey, Study #7454, November 2, 2004.

Indeed, these results suggest that the labor–Democratic Party alliance is likely to remain strong in future elections.

Nevertheless, as John Sweeney conceded shortly after the 2004 election, labor will "have to do more" in future elections (Gruenberg 2004). Yet the 2004 election makes clear that unions have done about as much as possible with its current membership levels. Union turnout was very high and union household support for progressive candidates and issues was extremely strong. The failure of labor to do more in the 2004 election was simply that there were not enough union households. As stressed throughout this book, organizing more workers is thus essential to the future of organized labor in American politics.

Appendix

My goal in writing this book was to provide a comprehensive account of the state of organized labor in congressional politics since the election of John Sweeney as president of the AFL-CIO. I considered a variety of approaches to address this subject, including both an assessment of union members' political attitudes and behavior and a systematic analysis of the effect of labor union campaign activities in congressional elections and on labor legislation. I attempted to address several questions: (1) Have union members' attitudes become more favorable toward labor unions and the Democratic Party since Sweeney's election? (2) Have union members become more politically active since Sweeney's election? (3) What effects have increased union grassroots expenditures and other union campaign activities had in congressional elections since Sweeney's election? (4) What effect has the recent AFL-CIO advertising campaign had in congressional elections? (5) What effects have the increased overall union expenditures and contributions had on congressional members' support for labor legislation?

Data Sources

The statistical analysis of union members' political attitudes and behavior in chapter 3 comes from data compiled for the American National Election Study. The specific data set used for the analysis from 1988 to 2000 comes from the 1948–2000 American National Election Study cumulative data file (see Sapiro, Rosenstone, and the National Election Studies 2001). The 2002 American National Election Study is the source of the 2002 data (see National Election Studies 2002).

The statistical analysis of the effect of campaign expenditures and contributions on congressional elections in chapter 4 comes primarily from data compiled by the Federal Election Commission. The analysis uses the FEC's candidate summary files for the 1988 through 2002 elections, which are available at ftp://ftp.fec.gov/FEC. These files contain a record for each U.S. House and U.S. Senate candidate for each election cycle. They include campaign finance information about the candidates, including their total campaign expenditures and contributions and expenditures from corporate and labor PACs.

Specific information on union grassroots expenditures is not included in the candidate summary files, but it is available in the FEC's detailed committee files on PAC contributions. The detailed committee files contain one record for each committee transaction. It includes one record for each single contribution or expenditure that a specific PAC made to a specific candidate. This record identifies the candidate and the total amount given or spent by the PAC. The file also provides a description of the type of contribution or expenditure, which includes normal checks, in-kind contributions, independent expenditures made on behalf of the candidates or against the candidate, and communication costs made on behalf of the candidates or against the candidate. The sum of each different type of contribution or expenditure for all union and corporate PACs was then computed for each congressional candidate and merged into the candidate file.

Expenditures classified by the FEC as communication expenditures served as this study's "grassroots" variable. Communication expenditures include expenses on phone banks, direct mail, and flyers. These types of expenditures are generally made to help mobilize members to participate in the political process, and thus serve as a reasonable measure for grassroots expenditures.

All dollar amounts have been adjusted for inflation to reflect 2002 dollars. This includes almost all of the money-related measures reported throughout this book. The source for adjusting all dollar amounts for inflation came from the Inflation Calculator located at http://www.westegg.com/inflation.

Information on district partisanship and the share of the vote earned by the candidates came from various editions of the *Almanac of American Politics* (1990 through 2004 editions). Measures of political experience for nonincumbents in the data came from information reported in various editions of *Congressional Quarterly Weekly* and the Center for American Politics and Citizenship. Information on incumbents' COPE scores came from the *Directory of Congressional Voting Scores and Interest Group Ratings* (see Sharpe 2000); and AFL-CIO, "Congressional Voting Record," http://www.aflcio.org/issues/legislativealerts/votes/index.cfm.

Finally, information on union density came from Hirsch, Macpherson, and Vroman (2001). These estimates provide a breakdown of union density at the state level. Of course, a preferable measure would have been to obtain union density information at the congressional district level. However, the state-level measure constructed by Hirsch and colleagues is based on the U.S. Census Current Population Survey, and unfortunately, the CPS does not identify congressional districts. Box-Steffensmeier, Arnold, and Zorn (1997) created a measure of union density for the congressional districts in the 1990s through a rather elaborate procedure (see http://www.emory.edu/POLS/zorn/Data/readme.pdf). My analysis, however, includes the 1988, 1990, and 2002 elections, which involved different congressional boundaries than those specified in the Box-Steffensmeier, Arnold, and Zorn data. I considered creating my own measure for union density based on the congressional district boundaries drawn after the 1980 and 2000 Census. Unfortunately, this cannot be done for districts drawn from the 1980 Census, because the detailed Metropolitan

Statistical Area (MSA) breakdowns are not available before 1985. This left me with insufficient data to replicate the Box-Steffensmeier, Arnold, and Zorn measure. Furthermore, the state-level measure appears to be a reliable measure. The state-level measures of union density for the 1990s correlate at .92 with Box-Steffensmeier, Arnold, and Zorn's congressional district-level measure.

The data for the AFL-CIO's advertising campaigns during the 2000 and 2002 elections came from the Campaign Media Analysis Group. CMAG is a firm that uses satellite technology to monitor the transmission and broadcast of political advertisements in the top seventy-five media markets of the United States, covering 80 percent of the U.S. population. Its system tracks advertisements from the four major national networks (ABC, CBS, FOX, and NBC), twenty-five national cable networks, and local advertising in the nation's top markets. The data provide information about the number and costs of each advertisement. Researchers at the University of Wisconsin provided additional information to the data by coding the style and content of each advertisement (for more information, see http://www.polisci.wisc.edu/tvadvertising/).

The CMAG data break all information by the seventy-five media markets. To merge this information into the congressional candidate file, I matched all congressional districts with their primary media market. I then used the number of AFL-CIO ads as my measure, rather than the costs, because the price of a television advertisement can vary widely across media markets. An advertisement in the New York City media market, for example, is twenty-nine times more expensive than the same advertisement in the Waco, Texas market (Herrnson 2004).

In addition to these various data sources, I interviewed David DiStefano, a representative with the political director of the Chamber of Commerce, on September 9, 1999. We discussed the Chamber's upcoming election strategy for the 2000 election. I interviewed John Pérez, the political director for the California Labor Federation, on September 5, 2000, about both the organized labor's efforts to defeat Proposition 226 and the primary victory of Hilda Solis over Democratic incumbent Mathew Martinez.

Data-Analysis Techniques

There were several difficult methodological decisions that arose during this project. The first major decision concerned the statistical technique for the multivariate analyses in chapter 4. I opted to use generalized least square (GLS) estimates instead of the traditional ordinary least squares (OLS) estimates because the nature of the data requires a time-series cross-sectional analysis. Using OLS for these data can produce error terms that are heteroskedastic, autocorrelated, and contemporaneously correlated (Stimson 1985). GLS analysis corrects for this problem.

I also considered using panel-corrected standard errors for chapter 4. Beck and Katz (1995) popularized the use of panel-corrected standard errors for time-series analysis for data with a limited number of panels with many time periods. However, the data in this analysis has many panels but relatively few time periods (just eight election cycles). In this instance, the GLS method is the more appropriate and preferred method (Poi 2003).

There is also the problem of omitted variable bias, which is a problem similar (but not identical) to simultaneity bias. This problem can lead to biased coefficients. However, my analysis includes several control variables that are known to influence congressional vote totals. The campaign expenditure variables, in particular, mitigate many of the problems associated with omitted variable bias. For a complete and through discussion on this issue, see Jacobson (1999, 190–192).

There has also been some discussion in the political science literature about using two-stage-least-squares (2SLS) regression for estimating the relationship between measures that account for campaign spending and candidate's vote totals. However, Jacobson has concluded that there is not a strong simultaneity bias in such models (Jacobson 1985). Moreover, Jacobson makes a convincing argument that 2SLS equations are very sensitive to the choice of instruments, and when improperly specified, can produce inaccurate results (Jacobson 1990). Jacobson (1990, 342) notes that finding the proper instrument would require a measure that affects contributions but does not independently affect the vote—an extremely difficult task. For these methodological reasons, I opted against using 2SLS estimates (for more information, see Jacobson 1990).

The equations in chapter 4 also separate Democrats and Republicans. This was necessary because of difficulties associated with multicolinearity. A full 99 percent of Republican congressional candidates received no union grassroots assistance. Because union grassroots assistance flows almost entirely to support Democrats and against Republicans, separate analyses were necessary. I opted to separate incumbents from nonincumbent candidates because of the significant differences in the dynamics of these campaigns (see Herrnson 2000, chapter 9). I considered separating the models further for the Sweeney and Kirkland periods; however, this reduces the number of cases in my analyses to a large enough extent that it prevents an analysis of the U.S. Senate. To keep the techniques and methods consistent throughout chapter 4 and preserve the Senate analysis, I opted not to separate the Sweeney and Kirkland periods into different equations.

The analysis in chapter 5 includes only two election periods—the 2000 and 2002 elections. CMAG was able to provide me with data on the AFL-CIO advertising campaign for only those two periods. Given that only two elections are part of the analysis, a time-series analysis was unnecessary. I relied on traditional OLS analysis for those estimates.

In chapter 6, I opted to rely on generalized two-stage least squares (G2SLS) estimates for the multivariate equations because of endogeneity problems associated with support for labor policies and union campaign assistance. Single equation models have been found to overestimate the effect of campaign contributions or expenditures on roll-call votes (Chappell 1981; 1982). I relied on G2SLS estimates rather than on 2SLS estimates because the data require a time-series cross-sectional analysis (see Achen 1986 for more information). The results of the first-stage equations for table 6.3 are presented in table A-1 of the appendix. The results of the first-stage equation for table 6.4 are presented in table A-2 of the appendix.

TABLE A.1 First-Stage G2SLS Regression of Union Contributions and Expenditures for House Democrats on Instruments

	COEFFICIENT	STANDARD ERROR
Corporate contributions and expenditures.	191***	.026
Union density	3,344***	570
Competitive district	25,662***	4,488
Opponent's corporate contributions and expenditures	.595***	.054
Constant	25,626**	10,714
(N)	(1,651)	

* p < .05, ** p < .01, *** p < .001.

TABLE A.2 First-Stage G2SLS Regression of Corporate Contributions and Expenditures for House Republicans on Instruments

	COEFFICIENT	STANDARD ERROR
Union contributions and expenditures	.721***	.116
Union density	-3.046***	556
Competitive district	15,223**	6,701
Opponent's union contributions and expenditures	.311***	.037
Constant	167,506***	8,991
(N)	(1,403)	

* p < .05, ** p < .01, *** p < .001.

Variable Definitions for Measures in the Multivariate Equations

Candidate has previous political experience: This variable designates whether the candidate had previous political experience. It is coded 1 if the candidate previously held elected or unelected political office and 0 if the candidate was a political amateur. Candidates with elected or unelected political experience are defined as those who previously held an elected office or those who previously ran for Congress, served as a party official, held an appointed government position, or worked on the staff of an elected official.

Candidate vote shares: This variable serves as the dependent variable throughout chapter 4. It is based on the percentage of the vote received by the candidate in the general election. Vote totals are based on information reported in the *Almanac of American Politics* (1990 through 2004 editions).

Competitive district: This variable designates if there was a competitive election. It is based on Herrnson's (2004) definition, which classifies a competitive election as a contest decided by 20 points or less. Competitive contests are coded 1. Contests decided by more than 20 points are coded 0.

Corporate expenditures and contributions: This variable is based on all corporate PAC contributions and expenditures made on behalf of the candidate and against the candidate's opponent. This includes contributions defined by the FEC as "normal checks" or "in-kind" donations (identified as "24K" or "24Z") that were made on behalf of the candidate. It also includes all monies spent for independent expenditures on behalf of the candidate ("24E") and against the candidate's opponent ("24A"), and communication costs on behalf of the candidate ("24F") and against the candidate's opponent ("24N"). The amounts were indexed for inflation to reflect 2002 dollars.

Democratic president in power: This variable designates an election year in which Bill Clinton was the sitting U.S. president. The variable is coded 1 if the election year was 1994, 1996, 1998, or 2000. It is coded 0 if the election year was 1988, 1990, 1992, or 2002.

Democratic president in power × midterm election: This variable is an interaction term that multiplies the measure for "Democratic president in power" and the variable for "midterm election."

Election year 2000: This measure designates that the contest was held during the 2000 election cycle. The variable is coded 1 if the contest was held during the 2000 election and 0 if the election was held during the 2002 election.

Expenditure advantage over opponent: The amount of money that the candidate's campaign organization spent in the election minus the amount of money that the candidate's opponent's campaign organization spent in the election (indexed for inflation to reflect 2002 dollars).

Incumbent-incumbent contest: This variable designates whether there were two incumbents competing for the same seat following redistricting. The contest was coded 1 if there were two incumbents facing one another in the general election and 0 otherwise.

Labor communications – opponent's corporate communications: This measure is the difference between the amount of communications assistance that union PACs provided for the candidate compared to the amount of communications assistance that corporate PACs provided for the candidate's opponent. The measure is based on the candidate's communication assistance from union PACs, which include all costs on behalf of the candidate ("24F") and against the candidate's opponent ("24N") minus the opponent's communication assistance from corporate PACs. All dollar amounts are indexed for inflation to reflect 2002 dollars.

Labor contributions – opponent's corporate contributions: This measure is the difference between the amount of campaign contributions that union PACs provided for the candidate compared to the amount of campaign contributions that corporate PACs provided for the candidate's opponent. The measure is based on the campaign contributions that the candidate received from union PACs ("24K") minus the campaign contributions that the candidate's opponent received from corporate PACs. All dollar amounts are indexed for inflation to reflect 2002 dollars.

Labor independent expenditures – opponent's corporate independent expenditures: This measure is the difference between the amount of independent expenditures that union PACs provided for the candidate compared to the amount of independent expenditures that corporate PACs provided for the candidate's opponent. The measure is based on all independent expenditures on behalf of the candidate ("24E") and against the candidate's opponent ("24A") minus the opponent's independent expenditures from corporate PACs. All dollar amounts are indexed for inflation to reflect 2002 dollars.

Labor miscellaneous expenditures – opponent's corporate miscellaneous expenditures: This measure is the difference between the amount of miscellaneous expenditures that union PACs provided for the candidate compared to the amount of miscellaneous expenditures that corporate PACs provided for the candidate's opponent. The measure is based on any remaining assistance not specified as a contribution, communication expenditure, or independent expenditure. The variable is based on the amount of this remaining miscellaneous assistance that union PACs provided for the candidate minus the opponent's remaining miscellaneous assistance from corporate PACs. All dollar amounts are indexed for inflation to reflect 2002 dollars.

Midterm election: This variable designates whether the contest for Congress occurred during a midterm election year. Elections held in 1990, 1994, 1998, and 2002 were coded 1. Election held during presidential years in 1988, 1992, 1996, and 2000 were coded 0.

Number of AFL-CIO advertisements: This variable is based on the number of advertisements that AFL-CIO ran during the 2000 and 2002 election cycles in the top seventy-five media markets of the United States. The ads include those that appeared on the four major national networks (ABC, CBS, FOX, and NBC), twenty-five national cable networks, and local advertising in the nation's top markets.

Open seat contest: This variable designates whether the candidate competed in an open-seat election (i.e., a general election with no incumbent). The contest was coded 1 if there was no incumbent in the general election and 0 if there was an incumbent in the election.

Opponent has previous political experience: This variable designates whether the candidate faced an opponent with previous political experience. It is coded 1 if the incumbent faced a challenger who previously held elected or unelected political office and 0 if the challenger was a political amateur. Opponents with elected or unelected political experience are defined as those who previously held an elected office or those who previously ran for Congress, served as a party official, held an appointed government position, or worked on the staff of an elected official.

Opponent's corporate contributions and expenditures: This variable is based on all corporate PAC contributions and expenditures made on behalf of the candidate's opponent and against the candidate. This includes contributions defined by the FEC as "normal checks" or "in-kind" donations (identified as "24K" or "24Z") that were made on behalf of the candidate's opponent. It also includes all monies spent for independent expenditures on behalf of the candidate's opponent ("24E") and against the candidate ("24A"), and communication costs on behalf of the opponent ("24F") and against the candidate ("24N"). The amounts were indexed for inflation to reflect 2002 dollars.

Opponent's union contributions and expenditures: This variable is based on all union PAC contributions and expenditures made on behalf of the candidate's opponent and against the candidate. This includes contributions defined by the FEC as "normal checks" or "in-kind" donations (identified as "24K" or "24Z") that were made on behalf of the candidate's opponent. It also includes all monies spent for independent expenditures on behalf of the candidate's opponent ("24E") and against the candidate ("24A"), and communication costs on behalf of the opponent ("24F") and against the candidate ("24N"). The amounts were indexed for inflation to reflect 2002 dollars.

Partisanship of the district: This measure is based on the two-party vote for U.S. President for the Democratic nominee in chapter 4. Democratic candidates who ran in 1988 or 1990 received the two-party vote that Michael Dukakis won in their state or district in the 1988 presidential election. Democratic candidates who ran in 1992 or 1994 received the two-party vote that Bill Clinton won in their state or district in the 1992 presidential election. Democratic candidates who ran in 1996 or 1998 received the two-party vote that Bill Clinton won in their state or district in the 1996 presidential election. Democratic candidates who ran in 2000 or 2002 received the two-party vote that Al Gore won in their state or district in the 2000 presidential election. In chapter 5, the analysis turns to Republican incumbents. Here the partisanship variable is based on the two-party vote for U.S. President for the Republican nominee. Republican candidates who ran in 1988 or 1990 received the two-party vote that George H. W. Bush won in their state or district in the 1988 presidential election. Republican candidates who ran in 1992 or 1994 received the two-party vote that George H. W. Bush won in their state or district in the 1992 presidential election. Republican candidates who ran in 1996 or 1998 received the two-party vote that Robert Dole won in their state or district in the 1996 presidential election. Republican candidates who ran in 2000 or 2002 received the two-party vote that George W. Bush won in their state or district in the 2000 presidential election.

Support for labor policies: This variable serves as the dependent variable in chapter 6. It is based on the incumbent's average COPE score for each session of Congress. The AFL-CIO reports annual COPE scores. The measure used in the analysis computes the average of the two annual scores from each session of Congress. When a member of Congress served only one year in a session of Congress, the score for that year was used.

Three or more candidates in election: This variable designates whether there were three or more candidates (including the candidate) on the ballot in the election. It is coded 1 if there were three or more candidates on the ballot in the election and 0 if the contest was a two-person race or an uncontested election.

Uncontested race: This variable designates whether the candidate faced an opponent in the general election. It is coded 1 if the candidate did not have an opponent and 0 if the candidate did have an opponent.

Union density: The percentage of each state's nonagricultural wage and salary employees who are union members. For more information, see http://www.unionstats.com. For information about the methodology, see Hirsch, Macpherson, and Vroman (2001).

Union expenditures and contributions: This variable is based on all union PAC contributions and expenditures made on behalf of the candidate and against the candidate's opponent. This includes contributions defined by the FEC as "normal checks" or "in-kind" donations (identified as "24K" or "24Z") that were made on behalf of the candidate. It also includes all monies spent for independent expenditures on behalf of the candidate ("24E") and against the candidate's opponent ("24A"), and communication costs on behalf of the candidate ("24F") and against the candidate's opponent ("24N"). The amounts were indexed for inflation to reflect 2002 dollars.

Notes

1. Introduction

1. Selvin 1969, 14.
2. The CIO was originally known as the Committee for Industrial Organization. It was renamed the Congress of Industrial Organizations in 1938, following its split with the American Federation of Labor (AFL).

2. A Different Direction for Organized Labor?

1. AFL-CIO, 1996, "Union Survival Strategies for the Twenty-First Century" (press release dated March 20). See http://www.aflcio.org/publ/press96/pr03203.htm.
2. Figures compiled by the author.
3. The U.S. Supreme Court declared the NIRA unconstitutional in 1935. However, the Wagner Act (formally known as the National Labor Relations Act), sponsored by Democratic Senator Robert F. Wagner, provided federal protection for workers to organize workers and bargain collectively.

3. Strength in Numbers

1. Galvin 1998.
2. The NEA, unlike the AFT, is not affiliated with the AFL-CIO.

3. Asher and colleagues (2001) report that union members typically exhibit more prounion attitudes and behaviors than members of union households who are not themselves members. Thus, a measure of only union members would potentially exaggerate the gap between union and nonunion respondents. I therefore opted for the more conservative test of examining union households rather than union members only.

4. Countering Business

1. Galvin 1998.
2. Totals include retiring House and Senate incumbents. Subtracting these members does not change the overall pattern presented in figure 4.1.
3. Independent expenditures do not include amounts spent on "issue" advertisements. Issue advertisements avoid expressly advocating the election or defeat of a specific candidate, and therefore are not subject to federal reporting requirements. The effect of labor's issue advertisements are examined in chapter 5.
4. GLS is a linear estimation method. See Gujarati (2003) for more information.
5. The source for this is the Center for Responsive Politics. For more information, see http://www.opensecrets.org/1998elect/dist_sector/98CO02sector.htm.
6. Average margin of victory compiled by the author.
7. Numbers compiled by the author. All dollar amounts were indexed for inflation to reflect 2002 dollars. Total union campaign assistance includes all direct contributions, in-kind contributions, independent expenditures, communication expenditures, and other miscellaneous expenditures on behalf of the candidate. Independent and communication expenditures made against the incumbent's opponent are also treated as expenditures on behalf of the incumbent.
8. A more complex multivariate statistical model was not possible for Democratic incumbents. As noted in this chapter, vulnerable incumbents receive higher levels of union assistance than do safe incumbents. Thus there is an inverse linear relationship between union campaign assistance and the incumbent's electoral performance, as measured by his or her vote share in the general election.

5. The Air War

1. Greenhouse 1996a, A20.

6. Laboring for a "Working Family" Agenda

1. Sweeney 1996, 107.

7. Conclusion

1. Montgomery 1987, 7–8.
2. Figures computed by the author.

8. Postscript

1. T. Kuntz 2004, section 4, page 2.

References

Achen, Christopher H. 1986. *The Statistical Analysis of Quasi-Experiments*. Berkeley: University of California Press.

AFL-CIO. 1996a. "Organizing, Mobilizing, and Reawakening Hope." AFL-CIO press release (August 26), http://www.aflcio.org/publ/press96/pr0826l.htm.

——. 1996b. "Sweeney Announces Sweeping Changes at the AFL-CIO." AFL-CIO press release (January 24), http://www.aflcio.org/publ/press96/pr0124.htm.

——. 1996c. "Stop Voting to Block a Minimum Wage Increase, AFL-CIO Ads Tell Congress This Week." AFL-CIO press release (May 20), http://www.aflcio.org/publ/press96/pr0520.htm.

——. 1996d. "Republicans Try to Silence the Voice of Working Families." AFL-CIO press release (October 11), http://www.aflcio.org/publ/press96/pr10092.htm.

——. 1998. "Grassroots Campaign by AFL-CIO Aims to Pass Patients' Bill of Rights." AFL-CIO press release (September 10), http://www.aflcio.org/publ/press98/pr0910a.htm.

——. 1999a. "Building to Win, Building to Last." AFL-CIO Web site, http://www.aflcio.org/convention99/sr15_building.htm.

——. 1999b. "Labor 98: Working Families Vote." AFL-CIO Web site, http://www.aflcio.org/labor98.

——. 2000a. "AFL-CIO: Immigration." AFL-CIO Web site, http://www.aflcio.org/publ/estatements/feb200/immigr.htm.

——. 2000b. "People-Powered Politics: Working Families Vote." AFL-CIO Web site, http://www.aflcio.org/labor2000/election.htm.

——. 2002. "The Union Difference Political Program for Working Families." AFL-CIO Web site, http://www.aflcio.org/issuespolitics/politics /fs_0202.cfm.

——. 2003a. "Manufacturing." AFL-CIO Web site, http://www.aflcio.org/issuespolitics/manufacturing/

——. 2003b. "Global Economy." AFL-CIO Web site, http://www.aflcio.org/issuespolitics/globaleconomy/

——. 2003c. "Social Security." AFL-CIO Web site, http://www.aflcio.org/issuespolitics/socialsecurity/

——. 2003d. "Minimum Wage." AFL-CIO Web site, http://www.aflcio.org/yourjobeconomy/minimumwage/

——. 2004. "Union Members Voted Overwhelmingly for Kerry." AFL-CIO press release (November 3). See http://www.aflcio.org/mediacenter/prsptm/pr11032004.cfm.

Allsop, Dee, and Herbert F. Weisberg. 1988. "Measuring Change in Party Identification in an Election Campaign." *American Journal of Political Science* 32: 996–1017.

American Labor Studies Center. 2004. American Labor Studies Web site. See http://www.labor-studies.org/Labor_Quotes.htm.

Anglund, Sandra, and Clyde McKee. 2000. "The 1998 Connecticut Fifth Congressional District." In *Outside Money: Soft Money and Issue Advocacy in the 1998 Congressional Elections*, ed. David B. Magleby, 153–169. Lanham, Md.: Rowman and Littlefield.

Ansolabehere, Stephen, and Shanto Iyengar. 1995. *Going Negative: How Campaign Advertising Shrinks and Polarizes the Electorates.* New York: The Free Press.

Aronowitz, Stanley. 1998. *From the Ashes of the Old: American Labor and America's Future.* New York: Houghton Mifflin.

Asher, Herbert B., Eric S. Heberlig, Randall B. Ripley, and Karen Synder. 2001. *American Labor Unions in the Electoral Arena.* Lanham, Md.: Rowman and Littlefield.

Axelrod, Robert. 1972. "Where the Votes Come From: An Analysis of Electoral Coalitions, 1952–1968." *American Political Science Review* 66: 11–20.

Ayres, B. Drummond, Jr. 2001. "Political Briefing; Unions Want to Copy New Jersey Strategy." *The New York Times*, December 9.

Bailey, Eric. 1998. "Labor Upset Prop. 226 by Focusing on Backers." *Los Angeles Times*, June 8.

Balz, Dan, and Mike Allen. 2002. "2004 is Now for Bush's Campaign; Early Advantage in Funds, Voters Sought." *Washington Post*, November 30.

Barlett, Donald L., and James B. Steele. 1996. *America: Who Stole the Dream?* Kansas City: Andrews and McMeel.

Barone, Michael, and Grant Ujifusa. 1989. *Almanac of American Politics*. Washington, D.C.: National Journal Group.

——. 1991. *Almanac of American Politics*. Washington, D.C.: National Journal Group.

——. 1993. *Almanac of American Politics*. Washington, D.C.: National Journal Group.

——. 1995. *Almanac of American Politics*. Washington, D.C.: National Journal Group.

——. 1997. *Almanac of American Politics*. Washington, D.C.: National Journal Group.

——. 1999. *Almanac of American Politics*. Washington, D.C.: National Journal Group.

——. 2001. *Almanac of American Politics*. Washington, D.C.: National Journal Group.

——. 2003. *Almanac of American Politics*. Washington, D.C.: National Journal Group.

Bartels, Larry M. 1993. "Message Received: The Political Impact of Media Exposure." *American Political Science Review* 87: 267–285.

Battista, Andrew. 1991. "Political Divisions in Organized Labor, 1968–1988." *Polity* 24: 173–197.

Baumgartner, Frank R., and Beth L. Leech. 1998. *Basic Interests: The Importance of Groups in Politics and in Political Science*. Princeton, N.J.: Princeton University Press.

Beck, Deborah, Paul Taylor, Jeffrey Stranger, and Douglas Rivlin. 1997. "Issue Advocacy Advertising During the 1996 Campaign." Annenberg Public Policy Center, University of Pennsylvania.

Beck, Nathaniel, and Jonathan Katz. 1995. "What to Do (and Not to Do) with Time-Series-Cross-Section Data in Comparative Politics." *American Political Science Review* 89: 634–647.

Beichman, Arnold. 1994. "Labor's Political Slippage." *The Washington Times*, December 6.

Bensinger, Richard. 1998. "When We Try More, We Win More: Organizing the New Workforce." In *Not Your Father's Union Move-*

ment: Inside the AFL-CIO, ed. Jo-Ann Mort, 27–41. New York: Verso.

Benz, Dorothee. 2004. "Sisyphus and the State on the Front Lines of Union Organizing." *Dissent* (Fall). See http://www.dissentmagazine.org/menutest/articles/fa04/benz.htm.

Berke, Richard L. 1998. "Labor Defeats Threat to Its Muscle." *New York Times*, June 4.

Berman, William C. 1994. *America's Right Turn: From Nixon to Bush.* Baltimore, Md.: Johns Hopkins Press.

Bernstein, Aaron. 2004. "Can this Man Save Labor?" *Business Week* (September 13): 80.

Bernstein, Aaron, Amy Borrus, and Steven Brull. 1998. "A Bazooka Aimed at Big Labor Backfires on the GOP." *Business Week* (June 15): 55.

Bernstein, Aaron, and Richard S. Dunham. 1998. "Unions: Laboring Mightily to Avert a Nightmare in November." *Business Week* (October 19): 53.

Bernstein, Irving. 1960. *The Lean Years: A History of the American Worker 1933–1941*. Boston: Houghton Mifflin.

Bok, Derek C., and John T. Dunlop. 1970. *Labor and the American Community*. New York: Simon and Schuster.

Box-Steffensmeier, Janet M., Laura W. Arnold, and Christopher J. W. Zorn. 1997. "The Strategic Timing of Position Taking in Congress: A Study of the North American Free Trade Agreement." *American Political Science Review* 91: 324–38.

Brecher, Jeremy. 1997. *Strike!* Boston: South End Press.

Brecher, Jeremy, and Tim Costello. 1998. "A 'New Labor Movement' in the Shell of the Old?" In *A New Labor Movement for the New Century*, ed. Gregory Mantsios, 24–43. New York: Monthly Review Press.

Bresnahan, John. 1998. "New AFL-CIO Ads Signal Strategy Shift." *Roll Call*, July 20.

——. 2002. "AFL-CIO Absent From Airwaves." *Roll Call*, October 21.

Bronfenbrenner, Kate. 2001. "Changing to Organize." *The Nation* (September 3/10): 16–20.

Bronfenbrenner, Kate, Sheldon Friedman, Richard W. Hurd, Rudolph A. Oswald, and Ronald L. Seeber. 1998. "Introduction." In *Organizing to Win*, ed. Kate Bromfenbrenner, Sheldon Friedman, Richard W. Hurd, Rudolph A. Oswald, and Ronald L. Seeber, 1–15. Ithaca, N.Y.: Cornell University Press.

Bronfenbrenner, Kate, and Tom Juravich. 1998. "It Takes More than House Calls: Organizing to Win with a Comprehensive Union-Building Strategy." In *Organizing to Win*, ed. Kate Bromfenbrenner, Sheldon Friedman, Richard W. Hurd, Rudolph A. Oswald, and Ronald L. Seeber, 19–36. Ithaca, N.Y.: Cornell University Press.

Brownstein, Ronald. 2000. "NRA, Unions Fight for Blue Collar Voters." *Los Angeles Times*, October 22.

Buhle, Paul. 1999. *Taking Care of Business: Samuel Gompers, George Meany, Lane Kirkland, and the Tragedy of American Labor*. New York: Monthly Review Press.

Bureau of Labor Statistics. 2004a. "National Compensation Survey: Occupational Wages in the United States, July 2003." (August). See http://www.bls.gov/ncs/ocs/sp/ncbl0635.pdf.

——. 2004b. "National Compensation Survey: Employee Benefits in Private Industry in the United States, March 2004." (November). See http://www.bls.gov/ncs/ebs/sp/ebsm0002.pdf.

——. 2005. "Union Members in 2004." Bureau of Labor Statistics press release (January 27). See http://www.bls.gov/news.release/union2.nr0.htm.

Burns, Peter F., Peter L. Francia, and Paul S. Herrnson. 2000. "Labor at Work: Union Campaign Activities and Legislative Payoffs in the U.S. House of Representatives." *Social Science Quarterly* 81: 507–522.

Butterfield, Bruce. 1992. "Labor Day Discontent." *The Boston Globe*, September 7.

Campbell, Angus, Philip E. Converse, Warren E. Miller, and Donald E. Stokes. 1960. *The American Voter*. New York: John Wiley and Sons.

Canon, Scott, and Steve Kraske. 1998. "Money Talks Loudly in Congressional Contest." *The Kansas City Star*, September 28.

Center for Responsive Politics. 2003. "2002 PAC Summary Data." See http://www.crp.org/pacs/index.asp.

Chappell, Harry W. Jr. 1981. "Campaign Contributions and Voting on the Cargo Preference Bill: A Comparison of Simultaneous Models. *Public Choice* 36: 301–312.

——. 1982. "Campaign Contributions and Congressional Voting: A Simultaneous Probit-Tobit Model." *Review of Economics and Statistics* (February): 77–83.

Christian Coalition. 2004. Christian Coalition Web site. See http://www.cc.org/mission.cfm.

Cillizza, Chris. 2003a. "Labor Group Rakes in $1.3M." *Roll Call*, September 15.

Cochran, John, and Rebecca Adams. "Fresh From a Set of Hill Victories, Can Labor Keep the Momentum?" *CQ Weekly* (September 1): 2004–2009.

Commons, John R. 1953. *History of Labour in the United States*. New York: Macmillan.

Congressional Quarterly. 1996. "Labor Targets." *Congressional Quarterly Weekly Report* (October 26): 3084.

Converse, Philip E. 1966. "The Concept of the Normal Vote." In *Elections and the Political Order*, ed. Angus Campbell, Warren E. Miller, and Donald E. Stokes, 9–39. New York: John Wiley.

Convey, Eric. 1998. "AFL-CIO Rallies for Proposal." *The Boston Herald*, July 19.

Cornfield, Daniel B. 1991. "The U.S. Labor Movement: Its Development and Impact on Social Inequality and Politics." *Annual Review of Sociology* 17: 27–49.

Cox, James. 2000. "CEO's Hail Passage, While Unions Vow Revenge." *USA Today*, May 25.

Dark, Taylor E. 1999. *The Unions and the Democrats: An Enduring Alliance*. Ithaca, N.Y.: Cornell University Press.

Delgado, Hector. 1993. *New Immigrants, Old Unions: Organizing Undocumented Workers in Los Angeles*. Philadelphia: Temple University Press.

Diemer, Tom. 1996. "Big Labor's $35 Million Ad Campaign Angers GOP." *The Plain Dealer*, May 12.

DiStefano, David. 1999. Representative, Chamber of Commerce. Personal Interview. September 9.

Dionne, E. J. 2000. "Lean Labor's Big Win." *The Washington Post*, March 14.

Dunlop, John T. 1990. *The Management of Labor Unions: Decision Making with Historical Constraints*. Lexington, Mass.: Lexington Books.

Edsall, Thomas B. 2000. "Unions Mobilize to Beat Bush, Regain House." *The Washington Post*, March 27.

——. 2003. "Labor Targets Nonunion Voters; $20 Million Turnout Effort Expands Effort to Regain Influence." *Washington Post*, February 27.

Eismeier, Theodore J., and Philip H. Pollock III. 1988. *Business, Money, and the Rise of Corporate PACs in American Elections*. New York: Quorum Books.

Erikson, Robert S., Thomas D. Lancaster, and David W. Romero.

1989. "Group Components of the Presidential Vote, 1952–1984." *Journal of Politics* 51: 337–346.

Ezra, Marni. 1999. "Still Bringing Home the Bacon: The United Food and Commercial Workers International Union." In *After the Revolution: PACs, Lobbies, and the Republican Congress*, ed. Robert Biersack, Paul S. Herrnson, and Clyde Wilcox, 94–101. Boston: Allyn and Bacon.

FEC. 2003. "PAC Activity Increases for 2002 Elections." FEC press release (March 27). See http://www.fec.gov/press/press2003/20030327pac/20030327pac.html.

Finkel, Steven. 1993. "Reexamining the 'Minimal Effects' Model in Recent Presidential Elections." *Journal of Politics* 55: 1–21.

Folkenflik, David. 2000. "Business Elects to Go Its Own Way." *The Baltimore Sun*, February 27.

Francia, Peter L. 2000. "Awakening the Sleeping Giant: The Renaissance of Organized Labor in American Politics." Dissertation. Department of Government and Politics, University of Maryland, College Park.

——. 2005. "Protecting America's Workers in Hostile Territory: Unions and the Republican Congress." In *The Interest Group Connection*, ed. Paul S. Herrnson, Ronald G. Shaiko, and Clyde Wilcox, 212–228. Washington, D.C.: CQ Press.

Freeman, Richard B. 1985. "Why Are Unions Faring Poorly in NLRB Representation Elections?" In *Challenges and Choices Facing American Labor*, ed. Thomas A. Kochran, 45–64. Cambridge, Mass.: MIT Press.

——. 1986. "Unionism Comes to the Public Sector." *Journal of Economic Literature* 24: 41–86.

Freeman, Richard B., and James L. Medoff. 1984. *What Do Unions Do?* New York: Basic Books.

Friedman, Milton, and Rose Friedman. 1980. *Free to Choose*. New York: Harcourt Brace Jovanovich.

Fritz, Sara. 2002. "Unions' PR Campaign Backfires." *St. Petersburg Times*, December 9.

Galvin, Kevin. 1998. "Labor Claims Victory in Elections." *Associated Press*, November 4.

George, Mary. 1998. "Udall Gives Strikers a Pep Talk." *Denver Post*, August 22.

Gerber, Robin. 1999. "Building to Win, Building to Last: AFL-CIO COPE Takes on the Republican Congress." In *After the Revolution: PACs,*

Lobbies, and the Republican Congress, ed. Robert Biersack, Paul S. Herrnson, and Clyde Wilcox, 77–93. Boston: Allyn and Bacon.

Gerstle, Gary. 2002. *Working-Class Americanism: The Politics of Labor in a Textile City, 1914–1960*. Princeton, N.J.: Princeton University Press.

Gimpel, James G. 1996. *Fulfilling the Contract: The First 100 Days*. Boston: Allyn and Bacon.

Goldfield, Michael. 1986. "Labor in American Politics—Its Current Weakness." *Journal of Politics* 48: 2–29.

——. 1987. *The Decline of Organized Labor in the United States*. Chicago: The University of Chicago Press.

Goldstein, Kenneth M. 1999. *Interest Groups, Lobbying, and Participation in America*. New York: Cambridge University Press.

Goldstein, Kenneth, Michael Franz, and Travis Ridout. 2002. "Political Advertising in 2000." Combined File [dataset]. Final release. Madison, Wis.: The Department of Political Science at The University of Wisconsin-Madison and The Brennan Center for Justice at New York University.

Gompers, Samuel. [1906] 1978. "Labor's Bill of Grievances." In *Labor and American Politics*, ed. Charles M. Rehmus, Doris B. McLaughlin, and Frederick H. Nesbitt, 94–95. Ann Arbor: University of Michigan Press.

Gopoian, J. David. 1984. "What Makes PACs Tick? An Analysis of the Allocation Patterns of Economic Interest Groups." *American Journal of Political Science* 28: 259–81.

Gottschalk, Marie. 2000. *The Shadow Welfare State: Labor, Business, and the Politics of Health Care in the United States*. Ithaca, N.Y.: Cornell University Press.

Grady, Sandy. 2000. "PA could be Forum for Gore vs. NRA." *The Charleston Gazette*, November 4.

Green, Donald Phillip, and Bradley Palmquist. 1994. "How Stable is Party Identification?" *Political Behavior* 16: 437–466.

Greenberg, Stanley. 2002. "2002 Congressional Vote by Demographic Groups." Greenberg, Quinlan, Rosner, Research Inc., November 12.

Greenhouse, Steven. 1995. "A Big Job for Labor." *The New York Times*, October 27.

——. 1996. "Despite Setbacks, Labor Chief Is Upbeat Over Election Role." *New York Times*, November 15.

——. 1997. "AFL-CIO Puts Recruiting at Top of Its Agenda." *The New York Times*, February 17.

——. 1998. "The 1998 Campaign: The Unions; Split in Endorsements Deprives Candidates of Advantage." *New York Times*, November 1.

——. 2000a. "Growth in Unions' Membership in 1999 was the Best in Two Decades." *New York Times*, January 20.

——. 2000b. "U.S. Labor Leaders Push Hard to Kill China Trade Bill." *New York Times*, May 14.

——. 2001. "New Political Field Challenges Labor Leaders." *New York Times*, February 12.

——. 2004. "AFL-CIO Plans to Spend $44 Million to Unseat Bush." *New York Times*, March 11.

Greenstone, J. David. 1969. *Labor in American Politics*. New York: Alfred A. Knopf.

Greenwald, Carol S. 1977. *Group Power: Lobbying and Public Policy*. New York: Praeger.

Grenzke, Janet M. 1989. "PACs and the Congressional Supermarket: The Currency is Complex." *American Journal of Political Science* 33: 1–24.

Grier, Kevin, and Michael C. Munger. 1986. "The Impact of Legislator Attributes on Interest Group Campaign Contributions." *Journal of Labor Research* 7: 348–361.

Gruenberg, Mark. 2004. "Union Leader Says 'We Have to Do More.'" Press Associates, November 3.

Gujarati, Damodar N. 2003. *Basic Econometrics*. New York: McGraw Hill.

Hart Research Associates. 1996. "AFL-CIO Post Election Study #4797." Hart Research Associates, November 6–7.

——. 1998. "AFL-CIO Election Night Study #5341." Hart Research Associates, November 3.

——. 2000. "AFL-CIO Election Night Study #6152." Hart Research Associates, November 7.

——. 2002. "AFL-CIO Election Night Study #6843." Hart Research Associates, November 5.

——. 2004. "AFL-CIO Election Night Study #7454." Hart Research Associates, November 2.

Hattam, Victoria. 1990. "Economic Visions and Political Strategies: American Labor and the State, 1865–1896." In *Studies in American Political Development*, vol. 4, ed. Karren Orren and Stephen Skowronek, 82–129. New Haven, Conn.: Yale University Press.

Heberlig, Eric S. 1999. "Coordinating Issues and Elections: Organized Labor in the Republican Era." *The American Review of Politics* 20: 163–180

Herrnson, Paul S. 2004. *Congressional Elections: Campaigning at Home and in Washington*. 4th ed. Washington, D.C.: CQ Press.

Hirsch, Barry T., David A. Macpherson, and Wayne G. Vroman. 2001. "Estimates of Union Density by State." *Monthly Labor Review* 124: 51–55.

Hoffman, Kathy Barks. 2000. "Unions, Blacks Helped Democrats Gain in the Senate." *The Record*, December 3.

Holbrook, Thomas M. 1996. *Do Campaigns Matter?* Thousands Oaks, Calif.: Sage Publications.

ILR. 2003. "Trade Union Membership." See http://www.ilr.cornell.edu/library/downloads/FAQ/UNIONSTATS2002.pdf.

Jacobson, Gary C. 1985. "Money and Votes Reconsidered: Congressional Elections, 1972–1982." *Public Choice* 47: 7–62.

——. 1990. "The Effects of Campaign Spending in House Elections: New Evidence for Old Arguments." *American Journal of Political Science* 34: 334–362.

——. 1999. "The Effects of the AFL-CIO's 'Voter Education' Campaigns on the 1996 House Elections." *Journal of Politics* 61: 185–194.

——. 2001. *The Politics of Congressional Elections*. New York: Longman.

Jamieson, Kathleen Hall. 2001. "Issue Advertising in the 1999–2000 Election Cycle." See http://www.appcpenn.org/ISSUEADS/02_01_2001_1999-2000issueadvocacy.pdf.

Jansen, Bart. 2002. "Familiar Fuel Heats Campaigns." *Portland Press Herald*, October 6.

Jenkins, J., and B. Brents. 1989. "Social Protest, Hegemonic Competition, and Social Reform: A Political Struggle Interpretation of the Origins of the American Welfare State." *American Sociological Review* 54: 891–909.

Johnson, David Cay. 1999. "Gap Between Rich and Poor Found Substantially Wider." *New York Times*, September 5.

Johnston, Paul. 2001. "Organize for What? The Resurgence of Labor as a Citizenship Movement." In *Rekindling the Movement: Labor's Quest for Relevance in the Twenty-first Century*, ed. Lowell Turner, Harry C. Katz, and Richard W. Hurd, 27–58. Ithaca, N.Y.: Cornell University Press.

Jordan, Lara Jakes. 2002. "Gekas, Holden Campaign on Last Day in Critical U.S. House Race." *The Associated Press State & Local Wire*, November 5.

Judis, John B. 1998. "New Labor, New Democrats." *The American Prospect* (September–October): 12.

——. 2001. "John Sweeney in Trouble. Labor's Lost Love." *The New Republic* (June 25).

Judis, John B., and Ruy Texeira. 2002. *The Emerging Democratic Majority*. New York: Scribner.

Juravich, Tom, and Kate Bronfenbrenner. 1998. "Preparing for the Worst: Organizing and Staying Organized in the Public Sector." In *Organizing to Win*, ed. Kate Bronfenbrenner, Sheldon Friedman, Richard W. Hurd, Rudolph A. Oswald, and Richard L. Seeber, 261–282. Ithaca, N.Y.: Cornell University Press.

Kaden, Lewis B., Eugene Keilen, Carol O'Cleireacain, and Bruce Simon. 1999. *What's Next for Organized Labor?* New York: The Century Foundation Press.

Karson, Marc. 1978. "The National Labor Union and the Knights of Labor." In *Labor and American Politics*, ed. Charles M. Rehmus, Doris B. McLaughlin, and Frederick H. Nesbitt, 68–74. Ann Arbor: University of Michigan Press.

Katz, Harry C. 2001. "Afterword: Whither the American Labor Movement?" In *Rekindling the Movement: Labor's Quest for Relevance in the Twenty-first Century*, ed. Lowell Turner, Harry C. Katz, and Richard W. Hurd, 339–349. Ithaca, N.Y.: Cornell University Press.

Kau, James, Donald Keenan, and Paul H. Rubin. 1982. "A General Equilibrium Model of Congressional Voting." *Quarterly Journal of Economics* 97: 271–93.

Kau, James, and Paul H. Rubin. 1981. "The Impact of Labor Unions on the Passage of Economic Legislation." *Journal of Labor Research* 2: 133–145.

Kearney, Richard C. 1982. "Public Employee Unionization and Collective Bargaining in the Southeast." *Southern Review of Public Administration* 5: 477–499.

——. 1992. *Labor Relations in the Public Sector*. New York: Marcel Dekker.

Kosterlitz, Julie. 1999. "Searching for New Labor." *National Journal* (September 4): 2470–2477.

Kruger, John. 2000. "Business Group Unveils New Grassroots Operation." *The Hill* (January 26): 35.

Kuntz, Tom. 2004. "The Most Important Article in Our History." *New York Times*, September 5.

Kurtz, Howard. 1998. "Democrats Chase Voters with a Safety Net;

Candidates Nationwide Hammer Republicans on Ensuring Social Security's Future." *Washington Post*, October 28.

Labor Research Association. 2000. "Union Voters in Key States Helped Al Gore Win Popular Vote." November 15. See http://www.labor-research.org/story.php?id = 200.

Lambro, Donald. 1998. "AFL-CIO's Election Day Effort Paid Off Big for Democrats." *Washington Times*, November 5.

Langbein, Laura. 1986. "Money and Access: Some Empirical Evidence." *Journal of Politics* 48: 1054–1062.

Lawrence, Jill, and Jim Drinkard. 1998. "Getting Out the Vote." *USA Today*, October 29.

Levi, Margaret. 2003. "Organizing Power: The Prospects for an American Labor Movement." *Perspectives on Politics* 1: 45–68.

Lichtenstein, Nelson. 1998. "Roll the Union On; Rebuilding the Labor Movement." *Institute for Public Affairs* (October 18): 18.

——. 1999. "American Trade Unions and the 'Labor Question.'" In *What's Next for Organized Labor?*, 59–108. New York: The Century Foundation Press.

——. 2002. *State of the Union: A Century of American Labor*. Princeton, N.J.: Princeton University Press.

Lindblom, Charles. 1977. *Politics and Markets*. New York: Basic Books.

Lipset, Seymour Martin, and Ivan Katchanovski. 2001. "The Future of Private Sector Unions." *Journal of Labor Research* 22: 229–244.

Love, Alice Ann. 1998. "Ad Blitz Sets the Stage as Congress Debates Patients' Bill of Rights." *The Buffalo News*, July 21.

Machlup, Fritz. 1952. *The Political Economy of Monopoly*. Baltimore, Md.: Johns Hopkins University Press.

Magleby, David B. 2000. "Interest-Group Election Ads." In *Outside Money: Soft Money and Issue Advocacy in the 1998 Congressional Elections*, ed. David B. Magleby, 41–61. Lanham, Md.: Rowman and Littlefield.

Magleby, David B., and J. Quinn Monson. 2003. "The Last Hurrah? Soft Money and Issue Advocacy in the 2002 Congressional Elections." In *The Last Hurrah? Soft Money and Issue Advocacy in the 2002 Congressional Elections*, 1–53. Provo, Utah: Center for the Study of Elections and Democracy.

Mantsios, Gregory. 1998. "Introduction." In *A New Labor Movement for the New Century*, ed. Gregory Mantsios, xi–xviii. New York: Monthly Review Press.

Marks, G. 1989. *Unions in Politics: Britain, Germany, and the United States in the Nineteenth and Early Twentieth Centuries*. Princeton, N.J.: Princeton University Press.

Masters, Marrick F., and John Thomas Delaney. 1987. "Union Political Activities: A Review of the Empirical Literature." *Industrial and Labor Relations Review* 40: 336–353.

Masters, Marrick F., and Asghar Zardkoohi. 1986. "The Determinants of Labor PAC Allocations to Legislators." *Industrial Relations* 25: 328–338.

May, A. L. 1996. "Redistricting Threatens GOP Seat." *The Atlanta Journal and Constitution*, July 30.

Mazzocchi, Tony. 1998. "Building A Party of Our Own." In *A New Labor Movement for the New Century*, ed. Gregory Mantsios, 243–253. New York: Monthly Review Press.

McCarron, Douglas. 2001. "Carpenters' Union Pulls Out of AFL-CIO." Press release. See http://www.nwlaborpress.org/4-6-01Carpenters.html.

Meckler, Laura. 2000a. "AFL-CIO Spending Heavily to Criticize Bush." *The Associated Press State & Local Wire*, September 26.

——. 2000b. "AFL-CIO Begins TV Ads in Five Districts." *The Associated Press State & Local Wire*, July 21.

Mecoy, Laura. 2000. "Immigrant Janitors' Strike Energizing Labor Movement." *Bee Los Angeles Bureau*, April 4.

Meyerson, Harold. 1998. "A Second Chance: The New AFL-CIO and the Prospective Revival of American Labor." In *Not Your Father's Union Movement: Inside the AFL-CIO*, ed. Jo-Ann Mort, 1–26. New York: Verso.

——. 2004. "A Tale of Two Cities." *The American Prospect* (June): A8.

Michels, Robert. [1910] 1962. *Political Parties: A Sociological Study of the Oligarchical Tendencies of Modern Democracy*. New York: The Free Press.

Milkman, Ruth, and Kent Wong. 2001. "Organizing Immigrant Workers: Case Studies from Southern California." In *Rekindling the Movement: Labor's Quest for Relevance in the Twenty-first Century*, ed. Lowell Turner, Harry C. Katz, and Richard W. Hurd, 99–128. Ithaca, N.Y.: Cornell University Press.

Mills, Mike, and Frank Swoboda. 1994. "After the Rout, It's a New Landscape for Corporate America; Deregulators See Their Chance to Set the Agenda in Congress." *The Washington Post*, November 10.

Moberg, David. 2002. "It's Payback Time: Labor-Backed Politicians

Are Being Asked to Return the Favor in Union Fights." *The Nation* (July 1): 19–22.

Montgomery, David. 1987. *The Fall of the House of Labor*. New York: Cambridge University Press.

Moody, Kim. 1988. *An Injury to All: The Decline of American Unionism*. New York: Verso.

——. 1996. "U.S. Labor Wars: Bottom to Top." *New Politics* (Winter): 81–91.

——. 1997. *Workers in a Lean World: Unions in the International Economy*. New York: Verso.

Mort, Jo-Ann. 1998. "Finding a Voice: The AFL-CIO Communicates." In *Not Your Father's Union Movement: Inside the AFL-CIO*, ed. Jo-Ann Mort, 43–54. New York: Verso.

National Election Studies. 2002. The 2002 National Election Study [dataset]. Ann Arbor: University of Michigan, Center for Political Studies [producer and distributor]. See http://www.umich.edu/~nes.

National Journal. 1998a. "Biographies of New Governors and New Members of Congress." *National Journal* (November 7): 2625–2655.

——. 1998b. "Snowbarger Targeted by Unions." *National Journal's House Race Hotline*, October 17.

National Rifle Association. 2004. National Rifle Association Web site. See http://www.nraila.org/About/NRAILA.aspx.

Nelson, Jack. 1996. "Gingrich Sees Broad Effort to 'Destroy' Him." *Los Angeles Times*, June 27.

Neustadtl, Alan. 1990. "Interest-Group PACsmanship: An Analysis of Campaign Contributions, Issue Visibility, and Legislative Impact." *Social Forces* 69: 549–564.

New York Times. 1984. "Teamster Complains About Stand on Mondale." *New York Times*, March 27.

Norman, Jim. 1998. "The Dog that Didn't Bark: The GOP Loses Ground Among the Affluent." *The Public Perspective* 10 (December): 110.

Nussbaum, Karen. 1998. "Women in Labor: Always the Bridesmaid?" In *Not Your Father's Union Movement: Inside the AFL-CIO*, ed. Jo-Ann Mort, 55–68. New York: Verso.

O'Donnell, Norah M. 1998. "Big Spenders: The Seven Hot Independent Groups to Watch in 1998." *Roll Call*, January 26.

Olson, Mancur. 1971. *The Logic of Collective Action*. Cambridge: Harvard University Press.

Pérez, John. 2000. Political Director for the California Labor Federation. Personal Interview. September 5.

Perl, Peter. 1987. "The Lifeline for Unions: Recruiting; Today's Issues are Markedly Different." *Washington Post*, September 13.

Perlman, Selig. 1928. *Theory of the Labor Movement*. New York: Macmillan.

Pessen, Edward. 1978. "The Working Men's Parties of the 1820's and '30's." In *Labor and American Politics*, ed. Charles M. Rehmus, Doris B. McLaughlin, and Frederick H. Nesbitt, 42–56. Ann Arbor: University of Michigan Press.

Peter D. Hart Research Associates. 1998. "Working Womens' View on the Economy, Unions, and Public Policy." In *Not Your Father's Union Movement: Inside the AFL-CIO*, ed. Jo-Ann Mort, 69–85. New York: Verso.

Piven, Frances Fox, and Richard Cloward. 1982. *The New Class War: Reagan's Attack on the Welfare State and Its Consequences*. New York: Pantheon Books.

Poi, Brain P. 2003. Statistician, Stata Corporation. Personal Interview. September 25.

Poole, Keith T., and Thomas Romer. 1985. "Patterns of Political Action Committee Contributions to the 1980 Campaigns for the U.S. House of Representatives." *Public Choice* 47: 63–112.

Potter, Trevor. 1997. "Issue Advocacy and Express Advocacy: Introduction." In *Campaign Finance Reform: A Sourcebook*, ed. Anthony Corrado, Thomas E. Mann, Daniel R. Ortiz, Trevor Potter, and Frank J. Sorauf, 227–239. Washington, D.C.: Brookings.

Quadagno, J. 1988. *The Transformation of Old Age Security: Class and Politics in the American Welfare State*. Chicago: University of Chicago Press.

Radcliff, Benjamin, and Patricia Davis. 2000. "Labor Organizations and Electoral Participation in Industrial Democracies." *American Journal of Political Science* 44: 132–141.

The Record. 1996. "GOP Claims AFL-CIO is Illegally Targeting Martini." *The Record*, October 8.

Rehmus, Charles M. 1984. "Labor and Politics in the 1980s." *Annals of the American Academy of Political and Social Science* 473: 40–51.

Riker, William H. 1982. "The Two-Party System and Duverger's Law: An Essay on the History of Political Science." *American Political Science Review* 76: 753–764.

Roman, Nancy. 1997. "'Fast Track' Flop, Party Potshot Hurt Clinton Among 'Friends'; President Angers House Democrats." *The Washington Times*, November 11.

Rosenstone, Steven J., Roy L. Behr, and Edward H. Lazarus. 1996. *Third Parties in America: Citizen Response to Major Party Failure.* Princeton, N.J.: Princeton University Press.

Rosenthal, Steve. 1998. "Building to Win, Building to Last: The AFL-CIO Political Program." In *Not Your Father's Union Movement: Inside the AFL-CIO*, ed. Jo-Ann Mort, 99–111. New York: Verso.

——. 2003. Notes taken by author at the conference, "The Last Hurrah?" National Press Club, Washington, D.C., February 3.

Rozell, Mark J., and Clyde Wilcox. 1999. *Interest Groups in American Campaigns: The New Face of Electioneering*. Washington, D.C.: CQ Press.

Salisbury, Robert H. 1969. "An Exchange Theory of Interest Groups." *Midwest Journal of Political Science* 13: 1–32.

Saltzman, Gregory. 1987. "Congressional Voting on Labor Issues: The Role of PACs." *Industrial and Labor Relations Review* 40: 163–79.

Sapiro, Virginia, Steven J. Rosenstone, and the National Election Studies. 2001. 1948–2000 Cumulative Data File [dataset]. Ann Arbor: University of Michigan, Center for Political Studies [producer and distributor].

Schlozman, Kay Lehman, and John T. Tierney. 1986. *Organized Interests and American Democracy*. New York: Harper and Row.

Seidman, Joel, Jack London, Bernard Karsh, and Daisy L. Tagliacozzo. 1958. *The Worker Views His Union*. Chicago: University of Chicago Press.

Selvin, David. 1969. *The Thundering Voice of John L. Lewis*. New York: Lothrop, Lee, and Shepard.

Sexton, Patricia Cayo. 1991. *The War on Labor and the Left: Understanding America's Unique Conservativism*. Boulder, Colo.: Westview Press.

Sharpe, J. Michael. 2000. *Directory of Congressional Voting Scores and Interest Group Ratings*, 3rd ed. Washington, D.C.: CQ Press.

Shaw, Daron R. 1999. "The Effect of TV Ads and Candidate Appearances on Statewide Presidential Votes, 1988–1996." *American Political Science Review* 93: 345–361.

Sherman, Mark. 1996. "Congressmen, Business Groups Respond to Unions' Ad Campaign." *Atlanta Journal and Constitution* (September 28).

Sherman, Rachel, and Kim Voss. 2000. "Organize or Die: Labor's New Tactics and Immigrant Workers." In *Organizing Immigrants: The Challenge for Unions in Contemporary California*, ed. Ruth Milkman, 81–108. Ithaca, N.Y.: Cornell University Press.

Simons, Henry C. 1948. *Economic Policy for a Free Society*. Chicago: University of Chicago Press.

Skocpol, Theda, and J. Ikenberry. 1983. "The Political Formation of the American Welfare State in Historical and Comparative Perspective." *Comparative Social Research* 6: 87–148.

Slaughter, Jane. 1999. "The New AFL-CIO: No Salvation from on High for the Working Stiff." In *The Transformation of U.S. Unions*, ed. Ray M. Tillman and Michael S. Cummings, 49–60. Boulder, Colo.: Lynne Rienner.

Slichter, Sumner H., James J. Healy, and E. Robert Livernash. 1960. *The Impact of Collective Bargaining on Management*. Washington, D.C.: The Brookings Institution.

Smith, Edward M. 2000. "Exec Shows Sour Grapes on Economy." *Chicago Sun Times*, September 4.

Sobieraj, Sandra. 1999. "AFL-CIO: Shifting Political Focus." *Associated Press*, October 11.

Solomon, Wendy E. 1998. "Unions Leading Attack on HMOs." *The Morning Call*, September 11.

Sorauf, Frank J. 1992. "Political Parties and Political Action Committees: Two Life Cycles." *Arizona Law Review* 22: 445–463.

Stern, Andrew L. 2001. "Replies." *The Nation* (September 3/10): 23–24.

Stevens, Allison. 2002. "Big Labor to Take Aim at Free Traders." *The Hill* (May 22): 1.

Stimson, James. 1985. "Regression in Space and Time: A Statistical Essay." *American Journal of Political Science* 29: 914–947.

St. Louis Post Dispatch. 1999. "Largest Union Victory in Decades is a Big Boost for Labor." *St. Louis Post Dispatch*, February 28.

Stranger, Jeffrey D., and Douglas G. Rivlin. 1999. "American Federation of Labor and Congress of Industrial Organizations (AFL-CIO)." Annenberg Public Policy Center, University of Pennsylvania. See http://appcpenn.org/issueads/profiles/aflcio.htm.

Sweeney, John J. 1996. *America Needs a Raise*. Boston: Houghton Mifflin.

Swoboda, Frank. 1995a. "Militants Shaking Up Labor's Ranks; Delegates Push AFL-CIO Candidates to Get Tough, Stem Decline." *Washington Post*, October 25.

——. 1995b. "AFL-CIO Elects New Leadership; Activists Challenger Vows to Remake Union." *Washington Post*, October 26.

——. 2000. "Labor Targets 71 House Districts in 'Watershed Year.'" *Washington Post*, February 16.

——. 2001. "Labor Offers Own Tax Plan." *Washington Post*, February 15.

Swoboda, Frank, and Thomas B. Edsall. 1996. "AFL-CIO Endorses Clinton, Approves $35 Million Political Program." *Washington Post*, March 26.

Tarrow, Sidney. 1998. *Power in Movement: Social Movements and Contentious Politics*. New York: Cambridge University Press.

Tasini, Jonathan. 1995. "Labor's Last Chance; What the Unions Can Do to Help American Workers—and Save Themselves." *Washington Post*, February 12.

Toner, Robin. 1996. "Battered by Labor's Ads, Republicans Strike Back." *The New York Times*, July 15.

Troy, Leo. 1994. *The New Unionism in the New Society: Public Sector Unions in the Redistributive State*. Fairfax, Va.: George Mason University Press.

Turner, Lowell, Harry C. Katz, and Richard W. Hurd. 2001. "Introduction: Revival of the American Labor Movement: Issues, Problems, Prospects." In *Rekindling the Movement: Labor's Quest for Relevance in the Twenty-first Century*, ed. Lowell Turner, Harry C. Katz, and Richard W. Hurd, 1–5. Ithaca, N.Y.: Cornell University Press.

Uchitelle, Louis. 1995. "Awakened Labor Federation Tries to Cope With Hostile Times." *The New York Times*, February 26.

U.S. News and World Report. 1977. "Today's Militant Union Leaders and What They're After." *U.S. News and World Report* (April 11).

Uslaner, Eric M. 1998. "Let the Chips Fall Where They May? Executive and Constituency Influences on Congressional Voting on NAFTA." *Legislative Studies Quarterly* 23: 347–371.

VandeHei, Jim. 1998. "AFL-CIO Slates $28 Million for House and Senate Races." *Roll Call*, March 30.

Victor, Kirk. 1994. "Friend or Enemy?" *National Journal* (November 5): 2575–2587.

Victor, Kirk, and Eliza Newlin Carney. 1999. "Labor's Political Muscle." *National Journal* (September 4): 2478–2482.

Vogel, David. 1989. *Fluctuating Fortunes: The Political Power of Business in America*. New York: Basic Books.

Wawro, Gregory. 2001. "A Panel Probit Analysis of Campaign Contributions and Roll-Call Votes." *American Journal of Political Science* 45: 563–579.

Weinstein, Joshua L. 2002. "AFL-CIO Ad Tries to Plant Doubts About Collins." *Portland Press Herald*, July 29.

Wells, Miriam J. 2000. "Immigration and Unionization in the San Francisco Hotel Industry." In *Organizing Immigrants: The Challenge for Unions in Contemporary California*, ed. Ruth Milkman, 109–129. Ithaca, N.Y.: Cornell University Press.

Wilcox, Clyde. 1994. "Coping with Increasing Business Influence: The AFL-CIO's Committee on Political Education." In *Risky Business? PAC Decisionmaking in Congressional Elections*, ed. Robert Biersack, Paul S. Herrnson, and Clyde Wilcox, 19–28. Armonk, N.Y.: M. E. Sharpe.

Wilhite, Allen. 1988. "Union PAC Contributions and Legislative Voting." *Journal of Labor Research* 9: 79–90.

Will, George F. 2003. "Will Union Leader Be Democrats' Kingmaker?" *Augusta Chronicle*, June 12.

Wolfson, Bernard J. 1996. "Labor Declares Election Victory; $35M War Chest Felt in Bay State; Labor Officials Declare Victory in Election." *Boston Herald*, November 7.

Wright, John. 1985. "PACs, Contributions, and Roll Calls: An Organizational Perspective." *American Political Science Review* 79: 400–14.

——. 1996. *Interest Groups and Congress*. Boston: Allyn and Bacon.

Yang, John E., and Clay Chandler. 1996. "Modified Wage Hike Plan Wins Praise From Armey; Working Families Would Get Subsidies Under Proposal." *Washington Post*, April 24.

Index